COLLINS

QUIZ

BOOK

Carol P. Shaw

HarperCollins*Publishers*

HarperCollins*Publishers*
P. O. Box, Glasgow G4 0NB
www.**fire**and**water**.com

Reprint 10 9 8 7 6

ISBN 0 00 472023 7

A catalogue record for this book is available from the British Library.

Printed in Great Britain by
Caledonian International Book Manufacturing Ltd, Glasgow G64

CONTENTS

HOW TO USE THIS BOOK

This book is simply designed and easy to use.

QUESTIONS
Each of 120 pages has a set of questions covering aspects of popular knowledge and culture. Ten of the questions fall into specific categories, while the eleventh in each set, the 'True or False?' question, can be used either as a tie-breaker or just as a regular question.

ANSWERS
The answers page-number for each set is flagged at the foot of its questions page. In some answers, especially in the 'True or False?' category, part of the answer appears in brackets. This is simply given as extra information and is not essential to answer the question correctly – although you can use it that way, if you want to give your quiz a harder edge.

Good luck!

SECTION ONE

THE QUIZ BOOK QUESTIONS

SETS 1 – 120

Food & Drink What did Snow White's wicked stepmother use to tempt her?

 Natural World What is Bovine Spongiform Encephalopathy more commonly known as?

 History How many of Henry VIII's wives lost their heads?

 Culture & Belief If a god was Cupid in Rome, what could he expect to be called in Greece?

 Stage & Screen How many different centuries did Edmund Blackadder appear in?

 Written Word In what town did Roy of the Rovers play football?

 Music On what road did Nellie the Elephant meet the head of the herd?

 Famous People The 1956 marriage of what two seeming opposites prompted the headline 'Egghead marries Hourglass'?

 Sport & Leisure Why would you be given a green jacket and a yellow jersey?

 Science & Tech What world-renowned scientist played himself in an episode of *Star Trek: The Next Generation*?

 True or False? The American inventor of the deep-freezing process was a Mr Birdseye; true or false?

ANSWERS: PAGE 131

Food & Drink — What did the Israelites eat in the desert?

Natural World — How high is an equine hand?

History — What Roman Emperor made his horse a senator?

Culture & Belief — Whose New Look caused a sensation in post-war fashion?

Stage & Screen — The folk tune *Johnny Todd* was the theme music to what ground-breaking British cop drama of the '60s?

Written Word — What classic English work of literature features The Summoner, The Man Of Law and The Wife Of Bath?

Music — Whose *Song of Joy* is the anthem of the European Union?

Famous People — What famous sleuth contracted gangrene from biting his tongue after stumbling on an uneven pavement?

Sport & Leisure — In what town do Raith Rovers play?

Science & Tech — What famous motor manufacturer invented the motor car?

True or False? — Sideburns were named after a prominent wearer, US Civil War General Ambrose E. Burnside; true or false?

ANSWERS: PAGE 131

Food & Drink The berries of what shrub-like plant are used to make gin?

 Natural World What is the Windy City?

 History Why did the royal family move from Saxe-Coburg to Windsor?

 Culture & Belief Where did Panama hats originate?

 Stage & Screen In the climax of what film does the male lead climb down the presidential faces at Mount Rushmore?

 Written Word Who wrote *Look Back in Anger*?

 Music Who wrote *Don't Look Back in Anger*?

 Famous People Whose journeys aboard *The Beagle* allowed some revolutionary theories to evolve?

 Sport & Leisure What BBC TV programme popularised snooker as a spectator sport?

 Science & Tech Where would you find a Plimsoll Line?

True or False? Scotland Yard was originally the name of a medieval house used by Scots kings visiting London; true or false?

ANSWERS: PAGE 132

Food & Drink
What did Jack Sprat refuse to eat?

 Natural World
What desert separates Egypt and Israel?

 History
How long did the Berlin Wall stand?

 Culture & Belief
What are the Society of Friends more commonly known as?

 Stage & Screen
What was the first full-length animated feature film?

 Written Word
Who are Michael, Gabriel, Uriel and Raphael?

 Music
Who, according to the Stranglers, 'got an ice-pick that made his ears burn?'

 Famous People
What Australian Prime Minister was said to have tweaked the Queen's bra-strap?

 Sport & Leisure
What country was home to Sir Edmund Hillary?

 Science & Tech
Whose relatively famous theorem has the formula $E = MC^2$?

True or False?
The Oxford–Cambridge University Boat Race has never ended in a dead heat; true or false?

ANSWERS: PAGE 132

Food & Drink   What is Port Salut?

Natural World   What are the aurora borealis also known as?

History   How many Elizabeths reigned as queen in Scotland before Elizabeth II?

Culture & Belief   What God-given gift did Moses receive at Mount Sinai?

Stage & Screen   Who played Moses in the 1956 film *The Ten Commandments*?

Written Word   What Irish politician wrote a spy novel called *The Riddle Of The Sands*?

Music   What are 'Hammersmith Palais, the Bolshoi Ballet, jump back in the alley and nanny goats'?

Famous People   What business, apart from the movies, did Howard Hughes make his millions in?

Sport & Leisure   What was the official name of the original World Cup?

Science & Tech   What was the first British jet airliner?

True or False?   The first non-white British MP was elected over 100 years ago; true or false?

ANSWERS: PAGE 133

Food & Drink
What classic ad featured an alien family laughing at a traditional Earth recipe?

Natural World
If the aurora borealis are the northern lights, what are the southern lights called?

History
How many amendments have there been to the US Constitution?

Culture & Belief
What would a Scotsman tell an Englishman to do with a quaich?

Stage & Screen
What is Bollywood?

Written Word
What miser lost his gold but found a treasure in his adopted child?

Music
Whose daughter was *My Darling Clementine*?

Famous People
What did Oscar Wilde consider to be the curse of the drinking classes?

Sport & Leisure
In what year did Mark Spitz win seven Olympic swimming golds?

Science & Tech
What explosive device was invented by Alfred B. Nobel, founder of the Nobel Peace Prize?

True or False?
The Queen holds UK passport number 1; true or false?

ANSWERS: PAGE 133

Food & Drink   What is the ingredient which turns curry yellow?

 Natural World   What natural feature is common to Tanzania, Uganda, Sudan and Egypt?

 History   Who was killed on the Ides of March?

 Culture & Belief   What date is the Ides of March?

 Stage & Screen   Whose undersea world was visited in *Calypso*?

 Written Word   Who did Hamlet tell to get to a nunnery?

 Music   What two '50s pop stars died in the same plane crash as Buddy Holly?

 Famous People   What famous divorceé once declared that 'One can never be too thin or too rich'?

 Sport & Leisure   In what events did Jesse Owens win his four gold medals in the 1936 Berlin Olympics?

 Science & Tech   Who invented the aqualung?

 True or False?   Three times more people were killed in the 1906 San Francisco earthquake than on the *Titanic* in 1912; true or false?

ANSWERS: PAGE 134

Food & Drink
What inhabitants of British waters are called the Silver Darlings?

 Natural World
What name was given to the Quaker William Penn's woods on the American east coast?

 History
What city saw the assassination that sparked the First World War?

 Culture & Belief
What would Jesus' astrological birthsign have been?

 Stage & Screen
What pink piggy pals first hit British TV screens in 1957?

 Written Word
Whose partner was Jacob Marley?

 Music
Who was the Beatles' first drummer?

 Famous People
Who said 'I love Mickey Mouse more than any woman I've ever known'?

 Sport & Leisure
What Lord was the famous cricket ground named after?

 Science & Tech
What is found on the Periodic Table?

 True or False?
Humphrey Bogart never said 'Play it again, Sam' in *Casablanca*; true or false?

ANSWERS: PAGE 134

Food & Drink

If it's Heavy in Scotland, what is it in England?

 Natural World

What is catgut traditionally made from?

 History

Who foresaw his country's civil war in the phrase 'A house divided against itself cannot stand'?

 Culture & Belief

What is bogyphobia a fear of?

 Stage & Screen

Name three of the five Tracy Brothers from *Thunderbirds*.

 Written Word

What was the name of Sherlock Holmes' smarter brother?

 Music

What song opened the first live broadcast of Radio 1 in 1967?

 Famous People

How did Mahatma Gandhi, Indira Gandhi and Rajiv Gandhi die?

 Sport & Leisure

Where is kabbadi most frequently played?

 Science & Tech

What British classic first went on sale in 1959 costing £496 19s 2d?

 True or False?

A granny, a sheepshank and a bowline are all parts of a chimney; true or false?

ANSWERS: PAGE 135

Food & Drink
What do you get if you boil sheep's offal, oats, suet and spices in a sheep's stomach bag?

Natural World
What deer is not actually a deer but a member of the caribou family?

History
What year saw slavery officially ended in the USA, to within five years?

Culture & Belief
What European head of state wears a crown but is not a monarch?

Stage & Screen
Who starred in a biopic of US husband-and-wife dance team Vernon and Irene Castle?

Written Word
Whose seductive dance before King Herod was rewarded with the head of John the Baptist?

Music
What American state is the home of country-and-western music?

Famous People
What did Leonardo da Vinci, Jack the Ripper and Horatio Nelson have in common?

Sport & Leisure
What are the chances of throwing a double-six with two dice?

Science & Tech
What is the seventh planet from the Sun?

True or False?
There are six counties in the province of Ulster; true or false?

ANSWERS: PAGE 135

Food & Drink What two foods originate in the Italian town of Parma?

 Natural World What is a shooting star?

 History What, founded in 330 BC, was the world's first state-funded scientific institution?

 Culture & Belief How much money would you gamble if you bet a brace of ponies?

 Stage & Screen What four-legged companion went with Dorothy from Kansas to Oz?

 Written Word If the Times came from London and the Herald from Glasgow, where did the Guardian come from?

 Music 'Satchmo' was the nickname of what jazz legend?

 Famous People What is the name 'Satchmo' short for?

 Sport & Leisure Who said in 1966, 'They think it's all over – it is now'?

 Science & Tech How did Valentina Tereshkova shoot to fame in 1963?

 True or False? James VI of Scotland and I of England wrote an anti-smoking tract in 1604; true or false?

ANSWERS: PAGE 136

Food & Drink

What did a million housewives say every day in the 1970s?

Natural World

What is the world's longest river?

History

Who was the first woman ever elected to the British Parliament?

Culture & Belief

Who is the patron saint of lovers?

Stage & Screen

What two actors have refused their Oscars?

Written Word

Who was the Fat Owl of the Remove?

Music

What chart-topping '80s band was named after a family friend of Mr Spock?

Famous People

Who ruled longest – Queen Victoria or Louis XIV of France?

Sport & Leisure

Who won snooker's 1985 world championship with the last ball of the final game?

Science & Tech

What is the world's longest single-span suspension bridge?

True or False?

Tupperware was invented by a Mr Tupper; true or false?

ANSWERS: PAGE 136

Food & Drink — What is the Greek pastry baklava sweetened with?

 Natural World — What is the world's second-highest mountain?

 History — What happened at 11:00 a.m. on 11 November, 1918?

 Culture & Belief — How many years would you be married if you were celebrating your tin wedding anniversary?

 Stage & Screen — Whose screen test reported 'Can't act, can't sing, slightly bald. Can dance a little'?

 Written Word — Who was Graham Greene's *Third Man*?

 Music — What was the opening song of the Live Aid concert at Wembley Stadium in July 1985?

 Famous People — Whose 1938 radio production of *War Of The Worlds* had thousands of Americans fleeing invading Martians?

 Sport & Leisure — Who won football's first World Cup?

 Science & Tech — What US politician was the first American to orbit the Earth?

 True or False? — Bagpipers run the risk of lung infections from bacteria which lurk inside their bags; true or false?

ANSWERS: PAGE 137

Food & Drink
What is the main ingredient in a Palestine soup?

 Natural World
What are Bailey, Malin and German Bight?

 History
What scholarly monarch was called 'the wisest fool in Christendom'?

 Culture & Belief
What does 'amen' mean?

 Stage & Screen
Who had a *Brief Encounter*?

 Written Word
Who created *The Simpsons*?

 Music
What famous Irish folk band did James Galway and Van Morrison record hit albums with?

 Famous People
Where was Thomas à Becket murdered?

 Sport & Leisure
What board game, invented in 1931, was first called Criss-Cross?

 Science & Tech
How long, to the nearest minute, does sunlight take to reach the Earth?

 True or False?
Adolf Hitler used his grandmother's name of Schicklgruber for several years; true or false?

ANSWERS: PAGE 137

Food & Drink Where would an American put a weenie?

 Natural World What American state has the nickname 'the Lone Star State'?

 History Who was the shortest-reigning English monarch?

 Culture & Belief What is the Muslim holy book called?

 Stage & Screen What was the birthday of George M. Cohan's *Yankee Doodle Dandy*?

 Written Word Who is older, Superman or Batman?

 Music What was the name of Elvis Presley's original backing band?

 Famous People What person was said to be the inspiration and namesake of the teddy bear?

 Sport & Leisure What would you use to play chemin de fer?

 Science & Tech If you had a painful patella, which part of your body would hurt?

 True or False? Adolf Hitler was a trained housepainter; true or false?

ANSWERS: PAGE 138

Food & Drink — What drink taught the world to sing in the 1970s?

 Natural World — What is the capital of Australia?

 History — Which side fired the first shot in the American Civil War?

 Culture & Belief — What was the only thing that remained in Pandora's Box?

 Stage & Screen — What cult '80s film had *Man in Motion* by John Parr as its theme?

 Written Word — What was Superman's original home town called?

 Music — Who is the most-played composer at the Proms – Elgar, Wagner or Beethoven?

 Famous People — Who was the original millionaire philanthropist who built and owned Skibo Castle in Sutherland?

 Sport & Leisure — In which sport would you encounter a jerk?

 Science & Tech — What is deoxyribonucleic acid better known as?

 True or False? — Margaret Thatcher was a member of the Labour Party for almost two years in her youth; true or false?

ANSWERS: PAGE 138

Food & Drink — What would you find in the middle of a Sussex Pond Pudding?

 Natural World — What is the world's largest island (excluding the continents)?

 History — How many Jameses were kings of Scots?

 Culture & Belief — What date was Jesus conceived on?

 Stage & Screen — What '60s children's TV show featured Vienna's Lippizaner horses?

 Written Word — What is Eric Blair better known as?

 Music — What did Judy Collins have in common with the Royal Scots Dragoon Guards?

 Famous People — What European leader used his presidential powers to check a takeover of his favourite brewery?

 Sport & Leisure — Which two teams met in the world's first international football fixture?

 Science & Tech — What elementary discovery was made by Crick and Watson?

 True or False? — *Sumer is Icumen In*, from the 13th century, is the earliest known musical canon; true or false?

ANSWERS: PAGE 139

Food & Drink
Who was said to have advised starving French citizens to eat cake?

 Natural World
What city which is a country is the world's smallest?

 History
Where was the Crystal Palace originally built?

 Culture & Belief
What religion believes in the balance of Yin and Yang?

 Stage & Screen
'As if by magic, the shopkeeper appeared' in what TV show?

 Written Word
What was Charles Dodgson better known as?

 Music
What city was Maria Callas' birthplace?

 Famous People
Who said 'In the future everyone will be world-famous for fifteen minutes'?

 Sport & Leisure
What does the TT in motorcycling's TT Races stand for?

 Science & Tech
What process, first used to preserve wine, now preserves milk?

 True or False?
Leonardo da Vinci sculpted the *Venus de Milo*; true or false?

ANSWERS: PAGE 139

Food & Drink — What drink is known as uisge beatha (pronounced 'ooskay baa'), meaning the water of life?

 Natural World — What country uses the zloty as currency?

 History — What event was the Crystal Palace built to house?

 Culture & Belief — What church recruits unwitting followers through posthumous baptism ceremonies?

 Stage & Screen — What town is Coronation Street in?

 Written Word — What writer turned down a peerage and the Order of Merit but accepted the Nobel Prize for Literature?

 Music — Who urged his listeners to *Keep Right On To The End Of The Road*?

 Famous People — Who was the second man to walk on the moon?

 Sport & Leisure — Who was Britain's first million-pound footballer?

 Science & Tech — What do the saxophone, the guillotine and the biro pen have in common?

 True or False? — Until the 19th century, Italian boy sopranos could be castrated to preserve their high voices; true or false?

ANSWERS: PAGE 140

Food & Drink — In what concoctions were the victims of serial killer Sweeney Todd said to have ended up?

 Natural World — What is the difference between a leopard and a panther?

 History — Who was the only US president to have been elected four times?

 Culture & Belief — What name was Ras Tafari better known by?

 Stage & Screen — What famous family lives in Ambridge?

 Written Word — What was Dale Carnegie's most winning and influential book?

 Music — Who lost her heart to a starship trooper in 1978?

 Famous People — What famous Crimea veteran was 'the lady with the lamp'?

 Sport & Leisure — How long does a 12-round boxing match last if it goes the full distance?

 Science & Tech — What number would an ancient Roman write as MI?

 True or False? — William Shakespeare wrote *Hamlet* as anti-Danish propaganda while England and Denmark were at war; true or false?

ANSWERS: PAGE 140

Food & Drink
What is the vegetable Americans call an eggplant known as in Britain?

 Natural World
What makes a humming bird hum?

 History
Who was the second Lord Protector of England, Scotland and Ireland?

 Culture & Belief
What religion reveres the god Krishna?

 Stage & Screen
What was the name of Powell and Pressburger's film production company?

 Written Word
Who did Gore Vidal call 'the Acting President'?

 Music
What conductor got classical music in Birmingham all shook up?

 Famous People
What politician was called 'the Uncrowned King of Ireland'?

 Sport & Leisure
At which Olympics did synchronised swimming first appear?

 Science & Tech
What is iron oxide more commonly known as?

 True or False?
English is the world's most-spoken language; true or false?

ANSWERS: PAGE 141

Food & Drink
What drink is produced around the Spanish town of Jerez?

 Natural World
Roughly how many species of insect are there in Britain – 1000, 10,000, 20,000 or 30,000?

 History
What is King John said to have lost in The Wash?

 Culture & Belief
What is the only surviving wonder of the ancient world?

 Stage & Screen
What time-travelling medieval wizard was dazzled by electrickery and the telling-bone?

 Written Word
In what street would you find Smiffy, Wilfrid, Danny and Plug?

 Music
What were the boys of the NYPD choir singing in *The Fairytale Of New York*?

 Famous People
Who was first to reach the South Pole?

 Sport & Leisure
What baseball player made at least one hit in each of 56 successive games in 1941?

 Science & Tech
How many degrees do complementary angles make up?

 True or False?
The vacuum cleaner was invented by a Mr Hoover; true or false?

ANSWERS: PAGE 141

Food & Drink
What is a calzone?

Natural World
What city could you look down on from Table Mountain?

History
What did Nelson lose at Tenerife?

Culture & Belief
What would you be studying if your subject was sinology?

Stage & Screen
What soap set in Spain failed to strike gold?

Written Word
What famous family lived at 50 Wimpole Street, London?

Music
What is the term for a group of seven performing musicians?

Famous People
What psychic shot to fame by repairing watches and breaking cutlery?

Sport & Leisure
Who was the first unseeded player to win the men's singles at Wimbledon?

Science & Tech
When, to the nearest three years, did the first daily air service between Paris and London begin?

True or False?
Snotra was the Norse god of Wisdom; true or false?

ANSWERS: PAGE 142

Food & Drink
What writer collapsed and died while mixing a mayonnaise?

Natural World
What would you be doing if you were playing possum?

History
Who was the last emperor of India?

Culture & Belief
Where in a church would you find a nave?

Stage & Screen
Where could Peter the Postman, Dr Mopp, Windy Miller and PC McGarry be found in the 1960s?

Written Word
What Irish-born writer created the land of Narnia?

Music
Who took the Lennon–McCartney song *Michelle* to number one in the UK charts?

Famous People
What revered all-American hero joined the Boston Tea Party and rode to warn of the arrival of the British?

Sport & Leisure
What Irish writer was the only Nobel Prizewinner ever to be listed in Wisden's *Cricketer's Almanac*?

Science & Tech
What chemical element is represented by He on the Periodic Table?

True or False?
Catholicism is the world's largest religion; true or false?

ANSWERS: PAGE 142

Food & Drink
What is the main ingredient boxty, colcannon and champ have in common?

Natural World
What is the world's biggest baby?

History
On what date did the USA celebrate its bicentennial?

Culture & Belief
Who was the first person to be killed in the Bible?

Stage & Screen
What Nobel-prize-winning dramatist had a *Long Day's Journey into Night*?

Written Word
What First World War poet wrote an *Anthem For Doomed Youth*?

Music
Who thought in 1977 that *Red Light Spells Danger*?

Famous People
Who claimed she lost her virginity as a career move?

Sport & Leisure
What Caribbean country entered a bobsleigh team in the 1988 Winter Olympics?

Science & Tech
What innovation in sound recording was invented in 1978?

True or False?
The century plant blooms only once a century; true or false?

ANSWERS: PAGE 143

Food & Drink

What is scampi made from?

 Natural World

What city was previously known as Byzantium and Constantinople?

 History

Who were 'overpaid, oversexed and over here'?

 Culture & Belief

What Israeli king did both Donatello and Michelangelo sculpt?

 Stage & Screen

What two antipodean wonders spoke in a language humans could understand?

 Written Word

What is the name of Dennis the Menace's dog?

 Music

What kilted singer asked *Donald, Where's Yer Troosers*?

 Famous People

Who declared 'I can resist everything except temptation'?

 Sport & Leisure

What city hosted the first Olympic Games of the modern era?

 Science & Tech

What would you be studying if your subject was virology?

 True or False?

Orson Welles and Rita Hayworth were husband and wife; true or false?

ANSWERS: PAGE 143

Food & Drink — Whose divine dinners consisted of ambrosia and nectar?

 Natural World — What country is Kathmandu the capital of?

 History — What was the last battle fought on British soil?

 Culture & Belief — Whose 1920s' ad campaign permanently changed Father Christmas' costume from green to red?

 Stage & Screen — Who wrote *A Streetcar Named Desire*?

 Written Word — What recollections make up the world's longest novel?

 Music — What top British band used to be known as Seymour?

 Famous People — What evangelical preacher supported Richard Nixon and prayed at Bill Clinton's inauguration?

 Sport & Leisure — How many balls are on a snooker table at the start of a game?

 Science & Tech — How many teeth does the adult human have?

 True or False? — By 1996, Britain's favourite food was still fish and chips; true or false?

ANSWERS: PAGE 144

Food & Drink — What is a rollmop?

 Natural World — What is the only man-made object visible from space?

 History — Who told the British government 'We only have to be lucky once – you will have to be lucky always'?

 Culture & Belief — Who was the son of King Uther Pendragon?

 Stage & Screen — Who feuded with the Montagues in *Romeo and Juliet*?

 Written Word — Who was *The Once and Future King*?

 Music — What former Yardbird joined Ginger Baker and Jack Bruce to form Cream?

 Famous People — What was Malcolm X's other diminutive surname?

 Sport & Leisure — What were the Commonwealth Games originally called in 1930?

 Science & Tech — What is the largest muscle in the human body?

 True or False? — A Mr Singer invented the sewing machine; true or false?

ANSWERS: PAGE 144

Food & Drink What is the sour ingredient in a whisky sour?

 Natural World What country occupied almost one-sixth of the Earth's surface until 1991, but does not do so now?

 History What organisation's motto translates as 'Evil Be To Him Who Evil Thinks'?

 Culture & Belief What is Siddhartha Gautama better known as?

 Stage & Screen What film features Holly Golightly?

 Written Word What is the name of Noddy's best friend?

 Music What did my true love send to me on the eighth day of Christmas?

 Famous People What was Harlean Carpenter better known as?

 Sport & Leisure What was the first year that professional players were invited to Wimbledon?

 Science & Tech How many hands does Big Ben have?

 True or False? A giraffe has the same number of bones in its neck as a human; true or false?

ANSWERS: PAGE 145

Food & Drink
Apart from appearing in the Bible, what do Balthazar, Methuselah and Nebuchadnezzar have in common?

Natural World
What would you be studying if you were a batologist?

History
When was the Prague Spring?

Culture & Belief
What does the word 'guru' mean?

Stage & Screen
Who declared his crew's intention 'to boldly go where no-one has gone before'?

Written Word
How many legs did Enid Blyton's Famous Five have altogether?

Music
Who are the Three Tenors?

Famous People
'Kissing her was like kissing Hitler'. Who was Tony Curtis describing?

Sport & Leisure
Who was the only woman competitor at the 1976 Montreal Olympic Games not to be given a sex test?

Science & Tech
What scientist was reputedly told by his schoolteacher 'You will never amount to anything'?

True or False?
The first person recorded as describing the British weather was Julius Caesar during his invasion of 55 BC; true or false?

ANSWERS: PAGE 145

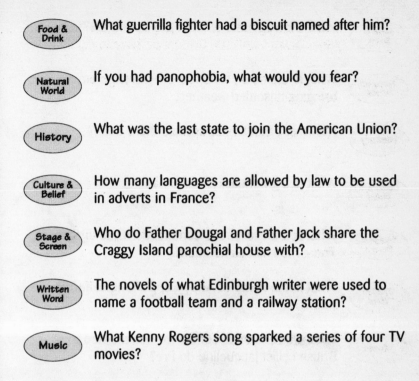

Food & Drink
What guerrilla fighter had a biscuit named after him?

Natural World
If you had panophobia, what would you fear?

History
What was the last state to join the American Union?

Culture & Belief
How many languages are allowed by law to be used in adverts in France?

Stage & Screen
Who do Father Dougal and Father Jack share the Craggy Island parochial house with?

Written Word
The novels of what Edinburgh writer were used to name a football team and a railway station?

Music
What Kenny Rogers song sparked a series of four TV movies?

Famous People
What head of state did the American CIA reputedly try to assassinate with an exploding cigar?

Sport & Leisure
Who was the first player to win the Wimbledon Men's Championship five times in a row?

Science & Tech
What fraction is used to express pi?

True or False?
An antimacassar was a special kind of mop used to polish Victorian tiled floors; true or false?

ANSWERS: PAGE 146

Food & Drink What did Yogi Bear steal in Jellystone Park?

 Natural World What is the name for a low-pressure system bringing unsettled weather?

 History How many British popes have there been?

 Culture & Belief What is a greenback?

 Stage & Screen What is unusual about Commander Data in *Star Trek: The Next Generation*?

 Written Word What is the name of Andy Capp's long-suffering wife?

 Music What world-famous conductor was married to British cellist Jacqueline du Pré?

 Famous People What is the Albanian Agnes Gauxha Bojaxhiu better known as?

 Sport & Leisure What sport was revolutionised by Dick Fosbury's flop?

 Science & Tech Who is known as the 'father' of the atom bomb?

 True or False? Cartoon character Popeye has a hamburger-eating friend called Wimpy; true or false?

ANSWERS: PAGE 146

Food & Drink What made Milwaukee famous?

 Natural World What cloud types are higher – stratus or cirrus?

 History What were the members of the Women's Social and Political Union popularly known as?

 Culture & Belief Whose commercials in the 1960s encouraged you to 'Put a tiger in your tank'?

 Stage & Screen What movie set in pre-war Germany was based on Christopher Isherwood's *Goodbye to Berlin*?

 Written Word What Japanese novelist committed hara-kiri after his attempted coup failed?

 Music Would you blow, pluck or hit a bazouki?

 Famous People What month was named in honour of Roman general Gaius Julius Caesar?

 Sport & Leisure Which famous US basketball team ran on court to their theme tune, *Sweet Georgia Brown*?

 Science & Tech What is a cock-up splint used to support?

 True or False? The safety razor was invented by a Mr Gillette; true or false?

ANSWERS: PAGE 147

Food & Drink
What ballerina gave her name to an Australian pudding?

 Natural World
How far would you have to journey to get to the centre of the Earth?

 History
Who is the First Lord of the Treasury?

 Culture & Belief
What New York State farm gave its name to a landmark event of the flower-power era in 1969?

 Stage & Screen
What FBI duo believe The Truth is Out There?

 Written Word
What cartoon strip, inspiring a TV sitcom and movie, was created by Charles Addams?

 Music
What would a bagpiper do with a chanter?

 Famous People
Who was the Young Pretender?

 Sport & Leisure
What sport developed from the first Hawaii Ironman Competition in 1974?

 Science & Tech
Until 1745, what were barbers officially able to perform as well as haircuts?

 True or False?
The pound note first came into circulation during the Napoleonic Wars; true or false?

ANSWERS: PAGE 147

Food & Drink
What was John the Baptist said to have eaten in the desert?

Natural World
Arches, loops, whorls and composites are all types of what?

History
How many members were originally in the Common Market?

Culture & Belief
What saint prayed, 'Oh Lord, make me chaste, but not yet?'

Stage & Screen
What grumpy pensioner had *One Foot in the Grave*?

Written Word
What science fiction author wrote the *Earthsea* trilogy?

Music
What band topped the UK chart in 1996 with *Spaceman*?

Famous People
Whose granddaughter Patti was kidnapped by the Symbionese Liberation Army?

Sport & Leisure
In which sport would you find soling, Flying Dutchman and tornado competition classes?

Science & Tech
What temperature does water boil at on the Fahrenheit scale?

True or False?
A sponge is an animal; true or false?

ANSWERS: PAGE 148

Food & Drink
What is the ingredient used to flavour Amaretto liqueurs and biscuits?

Natural World
What is the difference between lava and magma?

History
What did the Duke of Wellington describe as 'a close-run thing'?

Culture & Belief
Whose inscription in St Paul's Cathedral translates as 'If you seek a monument, look around you'?

Stage & Screen
What was experienced by the inhabitants of Cicely, Alaska?

Written Word
What recent conflict was described by an Argentinian writer as 'two bald men fighting over a comb'?

Music
Whose body lies a-mouldering in the grave while his soul goes marching on?

Famous People
Who was Anna Mae Bullock married to?

Sport & Leisure
Who is the only player to have scored a hat-trick in the World Cup final?

Science & Tech
How many stomachs does a cow have?

True or False?
Mahatma Gandhi was born in South Africa; true or false?

ANSWERS: PAGE 148

Food & Drink Bashed neeps and tatties are the traditional accompaniments to what Scots delicacy?

 Natural World How many time zones are there in mainland USA?

 History What were the colours of the first two British stamps?

 Culture & Belief What American terrorist group took their name from a line in a Bob Dylan song?

 Stage & Screen What does *ER* stand for?

 Written Word What novel, by a former teacher, charts the descent into savagery of boys marooned on a desert island?

 Music What band sang about *Waterloo Sunset*?

 Famous People What Argentinian doctor was boss of Cuba's national bank before going to Bolivia to start a revolution?

 Sport & Leisure Where was netball invented?

 Science & Tech If you suffered from hypotension would your blood pressure be too high or too low?

 True or False? Patagonia is a fictitious land from the works of 18th-century satirist Jonathan Swift; true or false?

ANSWERS: PAGE 149

Food & Drink — What is the minimum age for a malt whisky?

 Natural World — What does a limnologist study?

 History — What was William the Bastard's more common nickname?

 Culture & Belief — What would a yachtsman use a burgee for?

 Stage & Screen — What was odd about the TV detective pairing of Randall and Hopkirk?

 Written Word — Where did Kubla Khan a stately pleasure-dome decree?

 Music — Who wrote the opera *Madame Butterfly*?

 Famous People — What British leader was described as 'a very big woman, terrifying to look at, with a fierce look'?

 Sport & Leisure — Which three of the five Classic horse races make up the English Triple Crown?

 Science & Tech — What is the only organ in the human body capable of regeneration?

 True or False? — A Mr Fahrenheit invented the mercury thermometer; true or false?

ANSWERS: PAGE 149

Food & Drink — What makes jelly gel?

 Natural World — How many degrees of the Earth's surface does the sun travel across in one hour?

 History — Where in Europe did King Zog rule until 1946?

 Culture & Belief — What cult was invented by American science-fiction writer L. Ron Hubbard?

 Stage & Screen — What Boston bar did Sam run, Diane work and Frasier drink in?

 Written Word — What towns were the setting for Charles Dickens' *A Tale Of Two Cities*?

 Music — What country star is the world's biggest-selling performance artist?

 Famous People — What rotund ruler merited the nickname Tum-Tum?

 Sport & Leisure — In wrestling, which is heavier, bantamweight or featherweight?

 Science & Tech — What organism in bread makes it rise?

 True or False? — Richard the Lionheart introduced the handkerchief to fashion in the 14th century; true or false?

Food & Drink
What dish is traditionally associated with Easter?

 Natural World
What do the initials a. m. and p. m. literally mean?

 History
What is the world's oldest city?

 Culture & Belief
What dance phenomenon had its first airing at the 1994 Eurovision Song Contest?

 Stage & Screen
What group of bright young things frequent New York's Central Perk coffee bar?

 Written Word
Who wrote, 'Morality is simply the attitude we adopt towards people whom we personally dislike'?

 Music
What alphabetical band had a *Lexicon Of Love*?

 Famous People
By what childish name was Henry McCarty later and better known?

 Sport & Leisure
Which legendary golfer initiated the US Masters golf tournament?

 Science & Tech
What colour would an acid turn litmus paper?

 True or False?
Escapologist Harry Houdini died in a drowning accident during one of his tricks; true or false?

ANSWERS: PAGE 150

Food & Drink — What did the Romans mainly use salt for?

 Natural World — What are the two largest countries in the continent of Oceania?

 History — What year was the half-penny phased out?

 Culture & Belief — What would you be afraid of if you suffered from papaphobia?

 Stage & Screen — What house did Charles Ryder revisit in the book and '80s TV series?

 Written Word — What extraordinary book did Ford Prefect own?

 Music — Who was the lead singer of Thin Lizzy?

 Famous People — Who shot Billy the Kid in 1881?

 Sport & Leisure — What do Hamilton in Canada, Perth in Australia and Kingston in Jamaica have in common?

 Science & Tech — What metal was commonly known as quicksilver?

 True or False? — Three US presidents have resigned from office; true or false?

ANSWERS: PAGE 151

Food & Drink
The Roman poet Juvenal said people only wanted two things; one was circuses. What was the other?

Natural World
What is the most abundant metal in the Earth's crust?

History
What was the ship it was claimed that God couldn't sink?

Culture & Belief
What freedom fighter said 'I want to be the white man's brother, not his brother-in-law'?

Stage & Screen
His performance in what film won John Wayne his only Oscar?

Written Word
What five things did Old King Cole call for?

Music
Who sang about *A Boy Named Sue*?

Famous People
What millionaire philanthropist once claimed, 'The man who dies rich dies disgraced'?

Sport & Leisure
Which two British cities have hosted the final of the European Cup?

Science & Tech
How many numbers are there in a binary counting system?

True or False?
Tsar Peter the Great of Russia introduced the Japanese art of flower-arranging to the West; true or false?

ANSWERS: PAGE 151

Food & Drink — What months of the year are diners advised to avoid oysters?

 Natural World — What are pearls composed of?

 History — In what decade did native Americans become American citizens?

 Culture & Belief — How many pennies could you get to a pound before decimalisation?

 Stage & Screen — Whose army recruited Private Pike, Corporal Jones and Sergeant Wilson?

 Written Word — What did Solomon Grundy do on Saturday?

 Music — In what song did The Who hope they died before they got old?

 Famous People — Of what prime minister did Margot Asquith say 'He could never see a belt without hitting below it'?

 Sport & Leisure — What sport was the subject of the bestselling book, *Rare Air*?

 Science & Tech — What is the unit of measurement for pressure?

 True or False? — German physicist Heinrich Hertz also co-founded the well known car-hire company; true or false?

ANSWERS: PAGE 152

Food & Drink
What is unusual about the bread traditionally eaten at Passover?

 Natural World
What are the Chinook, the Mistral and the Sirocco?

 History
Which arm did Nelson lose at the Battle of Santa Cruz?

 Culture & Belief
Who was the first Christian martyr?

 Stage & Screen
What British TV first was achieved by *Stingray*?

 Written Word
What do seven magpies signify?

 Music
What band asked *Do You Really Want To Hurt Me?* in 1982?

 Famous People
Who make his fortune in the US with nickel-and-dime stores?

 Sport & Leisure
What trophy did the Wanderers and the Royal Engineers contest for the first time in 1872?

 Science & Tech
If you travelled at Mach 2, how fast would you be going?

 True or False?
Leon Trotsky was born in Dublin's Jewish district and taken to the Ukraine by his parents as baby; true or false?

ANSWERS: PAGE 152

Food & Drink
What Biblical character spent three days and nights as fish food?

 Natural World
What American state is Juneau the capital of?

 History
Who was the USA's first Catholic president?

 Culture & Belief
What two brothers with a talent for promotion coined the phrase 'Labour Isn't Working' in 1978?

 Stage & Screen
Who did King Kong fall for in the 1933 movie?

 Written Word
What was the significance of *Fahrenheit 451*?

 Music
What chart-topping duo did Vince Clark form after he left Yazoo?

 Famous People
What US president's previous jobs included that of male model?

 Sport & Leisure
Which is the fastest of all ball games?

Science & Tech
How many degrees' difference is there between 0° Centigrade and 0° Kelvin, to the nearest 10°?

True or False?
Allan Pinkerton, founder of the famous American detective agency, was a Glaswegian; true or false?

ANSWERS: PAGE 153

Food & Drink
What is unusual about the meat served in steak tartare?

Natural World
If the Greenwich meridian is at 0 degrees, what is at 180 degrees?

History
What was Al Capone eventually imprisoned for?

Culture & Belief
What type of clothing takes its name from an island in Shetland?

Stage & Screen
What cult '60s show featured TV's first inter-racial kiss?

Written Word
What did Robert Burns address as the 'Great chieftain o' the puddin'-race'?

Music
Name one of the two acts who have had a hit with *La Bamba*.

Famous People
What was the nickname of Manfred von Richthofen, the First World War's most successful pilot?

Sport & Leisure
Over how many holes is the British Open golf tournament contested?

Science & Tech
What is combined with copper to create bronze?

True or False?
In the past, carrots were white, purple and yellow, but not orange; true or false?

ANSWERS: PAGE 153

Food & Drink
What dish is known as a London particular?

 Natural World
What meteorological phenomenon did Charles Dickens call a London particular?

 History
Who was the victor of the Battle of the Little Bighorn?

 Culture & Belief
What are quasi-non-governmental organisations better known as?

 Stage & Screen
What was the name of the Lone Ranger's horse?

 Written Word
How many Brontë sisters were there?

 Music
What is the term for singing without any musical accompaniment?

Famous People
What would Napoleon have found it almost impossible to do tonight, or any other night, in bed?

Sport & Leisure
The governing body of which sport has its headquarters at Hurlingham in London?

 Science & Tech
Which is heavier, an imperial ton or a metric tonne?

 True or False?
Laws were passed in Elizabethan England to prevent commoners and peasants wearing hats; true or false?

ANSWERS: PAGE 154

Food & Drink — What is the main ingredient of laver soup?

 Natural World — When is Halley's Comet next due to pass near Earth?

 History — What nation was the first to use concentration camps?

 Culture & Belief — Where would you find the Book of Habakkuk?

 Stage & Screen — What was the title of Mickey Mouse's first celluloid outing?

 Written Word — What dramatist claimed that if there were no anti-Semitism he would not think of himself as Jewish?

 Music — Who had most hits simultaneously in the UK Top 30?

 Famous People — What monarch was officially insane for the last nine years of his reign?

 Sport & Leisure — Which runner held world records simultaneously at 1500 m, 2000 m, 3000 m and 5000 m in 1990?

 Science & Tech — What natural phenomenon would a seismograph record?

 True or False? — The cylinder lock was invented by a Mr Yale; true or false?

ANSWERS: PAGE 154

Food & Drink — Where did chilli con carne originate?

Natural World — What is the most populous native American tribe in the USA?

History — What was reportedly seen at Roswell, New Mexico, in July, 1947?

Culture & Belief — What does the word 'terracotta' mean?

Stage & Screen — What was the name of *The Godfather*'s Sicilian home village?

Written Word — Who wrote *The Playboy Of The Western World*?

Music — What spiritual song was the anthem of the 1960s' American Civil Rights Movement?

Famous People — Who ate poisoned cakes and was shot twice but only died after being tied up and thrown in a river?

Sport & Leisure — What sport was introduced to Britain in 1867 by a party of Caughnawaga Indians from Canada?

Science & Tech — If you knew your humerus from your gluteus maximus, what parts of your body could you identify?

True or False? — Writer Aldous Huxley taught George Orwell at Eton; true or false?

ANSWERS: PAGE 155

Food & Drink What, according to Dr Johnson, was eaten by horses in England and people in Scotland?

Natural World What is the world's highest waterfall?

History Which Robert do Bobbies take their name from?

Culture & Belief What would an American keep in his billfold?

Stage & Screen What is the family relationship between Francis Ford Coppola and Nicholas Cage?

Written Word Who wrote *The Godfather*?

Music What in the First World War went ting-a-ling-a-ling for you but not for me?

Famous People What was T. E. Lawrence better known as?

Sport & Leisure What is the exact imperial distance of a marathon race?

Science & Tech What size are the internal angles of an equilateral triangle?

True or False? Water drains down plugholes clockwise in the Southern Hemisphere; true or false?

ANSWERS: PAGE 155

Food & Drink
What, until the BSE scare, was Desperate Dan's favourite food?

 Natural World
What mammal's pregnancies last longer than any other on earth?

 History
What do the initials 'G.I.' stand for?

 Culture & Belief
What saint is represented by the emblem of a shower of rain?

 Stage & Screen
What classic British wartime drama won two Oscars for its star and creator, Noël Coward?

 Written Word
What writer said 'Other people have a nationality. The Irish and the Jews have a psychosis'?

 Music
What is an aria in an opera?

 Famous People
What fashion designer first came to prominence with her bondage wear during the punk era?

 Sport & Leisure
What weapon is used in the Japanese martial art of kendo?

 Science & Tech
Why is ethylene glycol added to car engines?

 True or False?
Scotch whisky is also produced in Japan; true or false?

ANSWERS: PAGE 156

Food & Drink — What, according to the nursery rhyme, are little girls made of?

Natural World — What country used to be called Siam?

History — Where did the Boxer Rising take place?

Culture & Belief — What does a Bat Mitzvah mark in the Jewish faith?

Stage & Screen — What film featured *Lara's Theme*?

Written Word — Who is credited with writing *Auld Lang Syne*?

Music — What opera is Bizet's most famous and popular?

Famous People — Who offered motor-car buyers any colour they liked, so long as it was black?

Sport & Leisure — What type of surface would a bandy match be played on?

Science & Tech — Which is longer, a nautical mile or a terrestrial mile?

True or False? — A dodecagon was a carnivorous dinosaur; true or false?

ANSWERS: PAGE 156

Food & Drink In what decade did sliced bread first appear?

 Natural World What causes the tides?

 History What fleet-footed IRA kidnap victim from the 1980s was never seen again?

 Culture & Belief Which of the 12 apostles was the tax-collector?

 Stage & Screen What film had *Moon River* as its theme music?

 Written Word What cartoon-strip family comprises Homer, Marge, Lisa, Bart and Maggie?

 Music Who were *Pretty Vacant* in 1977?

 Famous People What two historic martial heroes guard the gateway to Edinburgh Castle?

 Sport & Leisure How many fences are there in the Aintree Grand National?

 Science & Tech How many ounces are there in a kilogram, approximately?

 True or False? Kr is the symbol used to represent the element Krypton in the Periodic Table; true or false?

ANSWERS: PAGE 157

Food & Drink — What biscuit did West Country physician Dr William Oliver give his name to?

Natural World — How much skin is on the average adult male body, to the nearest square foot?

History — When was the United Kingdom founded?

Culture & Belief — What did the East End Revival Society become in 1878?

Stage & Screen — What orchestra played the theme to '70s Dutch cop drama *Van Der Valk*?

Written Word — Who is credited with writing *The Iliad* and *The Odyssey*?

Music — What famous West End musical is based on a collection of children's poems by T. S. Eliot?

Famous People — What utilitarian philosopher espoused the greatest happiness for the greatest number?

Sport & Leisure — Which US city plays host to the world's oldest annual marathon?

Science & Tech — How many litres of air does a fit adult take in with each breath?

True or False? — The lawnmower was invented by a Mr Budding; true or false?

ANSWERS: PAGE 157

Food & Drink — What prime minister's last words were 'I think I could eat one of Bellamy's veal pies'?

 Natural World — How many countries are there in Great Britain?

 History — What two Queens had Glasgow as their first home town?

 Culture & Belief — What item of fashion did Mary Quant invent?

 Stage & Screen — What military rank did James Bond hold?

 Written Word — Who wrote *Ulysses*?

 Music — Whose album *Arrival* topped the UK charts in 1977?

 Famous People — Who was manager of Manchester United at the time of the Munich Air Disaster?

 Sport & Leisure — Which is the oldest of the English Classic horse races?

 Science & Tech — What does vulcanisation do to rubber?

 True or False? — New York boasted the world's first skyscraper; true or false?

ANSWERS: PAGE 158

Food & Drink What British necessity did J. B. Priestley describe as 'the slow revenge of the Orient'?

Natural World How many inhabited Channel Islands are there?

History What does the monarch traditionally distribute on Maundy Thursday?

Culture & Belief What does etcetera mean?

Stage & Screen What rock star played a teacher in the film *Back to the Future*?

Written Word What English poet penned *The Mask Of Anarchy*?

Music What pianist and composer was the King of Ragtime music?

Famous People Who was the Irish–American choreography genius behind the Riverdance phenomenon?

Sport & Leisure What game is played on a diamond?

Science & Tech What was the invention which allowed multi-storey buildings to be built?

True or False? Chimpanzees are more closely related to humans than to gorillas; true or false?

ANSWERS: PAGE 158

What would you traditionally cook tandoori chicken in?

 What is England's highest mountain?

 What practice did former PM Harold Macmillan describe as 'selling the family silver'?

 Where in a car would Americans store their luggage?

 What was the stage name of Marion Morrison?

 What philosopher was Alexander the Great's teacher?

 What famous West End musical is based on the opera *Madame Butterfly*?

 Who urged the hippy generation to 'Turn on, tune in, drop out'?

 At which course is the Derby run each year?

 What vitamin deficiency causes scurvy?

 Baden-Powell started the Girl Guide movement as well as the Boy Scouts; true or false?

ANSWERS: PAGE 159

Food & Drink
To what favourite British dish are sodium chloride and acetic acid common additives?

 Natural World
What are the four provinces of Ireland?

 History
Who was shot and seriously wounded in Dallas, Texas on 22 November 1963?

 Culture & Belief
What is the Book of the Apocalypse better known as?

 Stage & Screen
Which of Marilyn Monroe's films ended with her version of *I Want To Be Loved By You*?

 Written Word
What British politician wrote *A History Of The English-Speaking Peoples*?

 Music
What performing company was most closely associated with the work of Gilbert and Sullivan?

 Famous People
What future prime minister declared, after winning a primary school prize, 'I wasn't lucky. I deserved it'?

 Sport & Leisure
The Colts football team and the Orioles baseball team are based in which US city?

 Science & Tech
What did the Royal Navy formerly carry on its ships to counteract scurvy in the crew?

 True or False?
Museum visitors in cultural centres such as Florence often contract Stendhal's Syndrome, a form of art fatigue; true or false?

ANSWERS: PAGE 159

Food & Drink — How many legs has a Bombay Duck?

 Natural World — What is the second-biggest city in Ireland?

 History — What was nicknamed 'The Iron Horse'?

 Culture & Belief — Who painted *The Laughing Cavalier*?

 Stage & Screen — In what film did Sherlock Holmes pursue Jack the Ripper through an establishment masonic conspiracy?

 Written Word — What Shakespearean play is the musical *Kiss Me, Kate* based on?

 Music — What was Abba's last UK number 1 hit?

 Famous People — What Californian Mama died of a heart attack in 1974 at the age of 32?

 Sport & Leisure — At which golf course is the US Masters held each year?

 Science & Tech — What is a celestial visible light spectrum better known as?

 True or False? — Henry Ford established the first automobile production line; true or false?

ANSWERS: PAGE 160

Food & Drink Where would you find a spirit safe?

 Natural World What famous 19th-century ornithologist published the elaborately illustrated *The Birds Of America*?

 History What war did the Light Brigade charge in?

 Culture & Belief What is the correct formal way to address an archbishop?

 Stage & Screen What was the connection between Darth Vader and the Green Cross Code Man?

 Written Word What school bully did George Macdonald Fraser make the hero of a series of humorous novels?

 Music When would you hear an intermezzo?

 Famous People 8th December 1980 was the day the music died for fans of what artist?

 Sport & Leisure Which two sports comprise the biathlon?

 Science & Tech What two colours lie at the opposite ends of the rainbow?

 True or False? It is possible to get to the end of a rainbow; true or false?

ANSWERS: PAGE 160

Food & Drink What is Mulligatawny?

 Natural World What group of individuals swear their ethical fitness in the Hippocratic Oath?

 History What street did the Great Fire of London start in?

 Culture & Belief Before 1752, on what date did the year begin in Britain?

 Stage & Screen What film has won more Oscars than any other?

 Written Word What was the name of Don Quixote's sidekick?

 Music What are 'whiskers on kittens, bright copper kettles and warm woollen mittens'?

 Famous People Rockers Richie Sambora and Tommy Lee have both married which beautiful blonde?

 Sport & Leisure How many times did Jackie Stewart win the Formula One World Drivers' Championship?

 Science & Tech What does the Mohs scale measure?

 True or False? Humans have more body hairs than apes; true or false?

ANSWERS: PAGE 161

Food & Drink
What country does chop suey come from?

 Natural World
Air is mostly composed of which two gases?

 History
Which organisation was the predecessor of the United Nations?

 Culture & Belief
Which is known as the senior service?

 Stage & Screen
What two actors played the part of Vito Corleone in *The Godfather* series?

 Written Word
What name was given to the survey of England ordered by William the Conqueror in 1086?

 Music
Who sang *(If Paradise Is) Half As Nice*?

 Famous People
What animator was responsible for *The Seventh Voyage of Sinbad* and *One Million Years BC*?

 Sport & Leisure
What sport's English governing body had W. G. Grace as its first president?

 Science & Tech
What disorder was called French Disease by the English, and English Disease by the French?

 True or False?
The tune of *God Save The Queen* is known in over 20 countries worldwide to different words; true or false?

ANSWERS: PAGE 161

Food & Drink What product was originally marketed as 'Liquid Beef'?

 Natural World Where is Queen Maud Land?

 History Who was Eisenhower's vice-President?

 Culture & Belief Who was the royal subject of a famous painting by Hans Holbein?

 Stage & Screen What director, famed for his westerns, has won more Oscars than any other?

 Written Word Whose masterpiece was the *Divina Commedia* (or *Divine Comedy*)?

 Music What did Molly Malone die of?

 Famous People *Help!*, *The Three Musketeers* and two of the four *Superman* films were the work of what US director?

 Sport & Leisure Who won the first University Boat Race between Oxford and Cambridge?

 Science & Tech What is said to have given Newton his first clue about the existence of gravity?

 True or False? The surface coating for non-stick pans was invented by a Mr Teflon; true or false?

ANSWERS: PAGE 162

Food & Drink
What food did the Aztecs use as currency?

Natural World
What was the first antibiotic?

History
What American became president of Ireland?

Culture & Belief
In the language of flowers, what is represented by a red rose?

Stage & Screen
What Stanley Kubrick film has he himself banned from British cinemas?

Written Word
Who wrote *A Clockwork Orange*?

Music
What does the musical term 'fortissimo' mean?

Famous People
The Magic Roundabout was created by the father of what Oscar-winning British actress?

Sport & Leisure
Which boxing heavyweights have held both the Olympic and professional titles?

Science & Tech
What does the computing acronym 'WYSIWYG' mean?

True or False?
St Vitus is the patron saint of dancers; true or false?

ANSWERS: PAGE 162

Food & Drink What were commuters urged to go to work on in the 1960s?

 Natural World What are aphids more commonly known as?

 History What Irishman became president of Israel?

 Culture & Belief How many labours had Hercules to perform to win his freedom?

 Stage & Screen Who is the only person called Oscar ever to have won an Oscar?

 Written Word In what special restaurant would you find Max Quordlepleen?

 Music What pub on the city road does the singer visit in *Pop Goes The Weasel*?

 Famous People What heart-throb was known as The King of Hollywood?

 Sport & Leisure How long does the famous Le Mans sports-car race last?

 Science & Tech How many constellations are there?

 True or False? New York was originally called Jorvik after it was founded by the Viking Leif Ericsson; true or false?

ANSWERS: PAGE 163

Food & Drink   What shape is farfale pasta?

 Natural World   What is the most northerly county in Ireland?

 History   Who called England 'A nation of shopkeepers'?

 Culture & Belief   What was the ship in which Jason and his followers set sail to find the Golden Fleece?

 Stage & Screen   What film depicted an RAF pilot suspended between a technicolour Earth and monochrome after-life?

 Written Word   Whose birthday is celebrated throughout the world on 25th January?

 Music   Who said 'follow the van and don't dilly-dally on the way'?

 Famous People   Whose catch-phrase was 'Just Like That'?

 Sport & Leisure   How many squares are there on a chessboard?

 Science & Tech   Where is the smallest muscle in the human body?

 True or False?   Pearls come in black, blue and green colours as well as white; true or false?

ANSWERS: PAGE 163

Food & Drink What does the term 'Napoleon Brandy' signify?

 Natural World What natural structure in central Australia is known by Aborigines as 'Uluru'?

 History Who was described as George Bush's best insurance against impeachment?

 Culture & Belief Name four of the seven virtues.

 Stage & Screen What Italian director made two films with *Once Upon A Time* in the titles?

 Written Word Who cut off Samson's hair?

 Music When is an opera a Grand Opera?

 Famous People What American president's father co-owned a movie studio?

 Sport & Leisure Nordic and Alpine are the two main categories of which sport?

 Science & Tech Which are older, veteran or vintage cars?

 True or False? The collective term for a group of apes is a 'parliament'; true or false?

ANSWERS: PAGE 164

Food & Drink
What day do Americans traditionally eat turkey?

 Natural World
What two things do bees collect?

 History
How long, to the nearest 10 years, did the Hundred Years War last?

 Culture & Belief
Name five of the seven deadly sins.

 Stage & Screen
What classic western was based on a story called *The Tin Badge*?

 Written Word
What was done to Count Dracula to make doubly sure he was dead?

 Music
What type of music would you expect to hear at the Grand Ole Opry?

 Famous People
Who replaced Glen Matlock on bass guitar in The Sex Pistols?

 Sport & Leisure
Which two teams contested the first cricket test match?

 Science & Tech
What is the only substance capable of cutting a diamond?

 True or False?
The British Constitution is stored in the library of the Houses of Parliament; true or false?

ANSWERS: PAGE 164

Food & Drink
What drink did the British in India take as an anti-malarial?

 Natural World
What bird has the largest wingspan?

 History
What famous World War One field marshal drowned off the north of Scotland in 1915?

 Culture & Belief
How long does Passover last?

 Stage & Screen
What unlikely POW movie featured Max von Sydow, Bobby Moore, Sylvester Stallone and John Wark?

 Written Word
What story was inspired by the sinking of the whisky-laden SS *Politician* in 1941?

 Music
Who had a UK top 10 hit in 1967 with a version of *Eidelweiss*?

 Famous People
Whose mammoth movie career ended in a sex-and-murder scandal in 1921?

 Sport & Leisure
Who was the last winner of BBC TV's *Pot Black* snooker championship in 1986?

 Science & Tech
What is a polygraph used to detect?

 True or False?
Louis Braille, inventor of readable type for the blind, was not blind himself; true or false?

ANSWERS: PAGE 165

Food & Drink
What is the difference between whisky and whiskey?

 Natural World
What is the fastest bird in the world?

 History
What war was income tax first introduced to finance?

 Culture & Belief
What Christian feast is celebrated on Whit Sunday?

 Stage & Screen
In what film would you find Sean Thornton, Mary Kate Danaher and Michaeleen Oge Flynn?

 Written Word
What two books did Robert Louis Stevenson's hero David Balfour appear in?

 Music
According to the song, what will we do 'though cowards flinch and traitors sneer'?

 Famous People
What music producer was famous for his 'wall of sound' production techniques?

 Sport & Leisure
Who was the first cricketer officially to be recorded hitting a six off each ball in a six-ball over?

 Science & Tech
How many carats are there in pure gold?

 True or False?
Vulcanised rubber was invented by a Mr Pirelli; true or false?

ANSWERS: PAGE 165

Food & Drink How many pints of beer are in a hogshead?

 Natural World What is known as the Staff of Life?

 History What Englishman was described as 'The Hammer of the Scots'?

 Culture & Belief How many rooms, to the nearest hundred, are in the world's largest palace in Brunei?

 Stage & Screen Where in London did the Wombles live?

 Written Word Sinbad, Aladdin and Ali Baba all originally appeared in what volume?

 Music What is the libretto of an opera?

 Famous People What is singer–songwriter Declan McManus better known as?

 Sport & Leisure In which Far Eastern country did the martial art of Taekwondo originate?

 Science & Tech How much would a ten-stone man weigh on Jupiter?

 True or False? Ernest Hemingway co-wrote the screenplay of the 1946 version of *The Big Sleep*; true or false?

ANSWERS: PAGE 166

Food & Drink Who invented the breakfast cereal?

 Natural World What country was also known as the Union of Myanmar?

 History How many brothers were there in America's Kennedy family?

 Culture & Belief What country has the dong as its major unit of currency?

 Stage & Screen What hugely successful film sparked a flood of disaster movies in the 1970s?

 Written Word What important manuscripts from the time of Jesus were discovered in an Israeli cave 50 years ago?

 Music What Spanish singing sensation used to play in goals for Real Madrid reserves?

 Famous People What age was Jesus Christ thought to be when he died?

 Sport & Leisure What are the two types of canoe used in international racing competitions?

 Science & Tech Do arteries carry blood to the heart or away from it?

 True or False? Flames spread more rapidly in a vacuum than in the open air; true or false?

ANSWERS: PAGE 166

Food & Drink What notorious gambler invented an easy-to-eat snack so he would not have to leave his card table?

Natural World What seas are linked by the Kiel Canal?

History What was the fate of the Stone of Destiny at Christmas, 1950?

Culture & Belief What colour does a Sikh bride wear on her wedding day?

Stage & Screen What Hitchcock film shows its action entirely from the viewpoint of a house-bound photographer?

Written Word What craft did Madame Defarge perfect in Charles Dickens' *A Tale Of Two Cities*?

Music What two singers had hits with *I Will Always Love You*?

Famous People Wagner's most famous fan was a politician who often played his music at rallies; who was he?

Sport & Leisure What four titles comprise tennis' Grand Slam?

Science & Tech Where would you expect to find a convection current?

True or False? Ho Chi Minh was told that he could become the world's greatest pastry chef if he gave up politics; true or false?

Food & Drink
What kind of fish is a kipper?

 Natural World
What is unusual about the Manx cat?

 History
Who beat whom in the Six Day War?

 Culture & Belief
What did the Romans call Manchester?

 Stage & Screen
What Christmas classic assured cinemagoers that 'Every time a bell rings, an angel gets its wings'?

 Written Word
Who was Thornfield Hall's mad inhabitant in *Jane Eyre*?

 Music
What dance craze was originally devised to promote the song *Achy Breaky Heart*?

 Famous People
What ballerina was *The Dying Swan* ballet specially written for?

 Sport & Leisure
Which country has dominated world-class chess?

 Science & Tech
What was the first hormone to be identified?

 True or False?
Skin is the largest body organ; true or false?

ANSWERS: PAGE 167

Food & Drink — What are the eggs of the sturgeon better known as?

 Natural World — Where would you find the Forbidden City?

 History — What French Protestant changed his religion to become king, declaring 'Paris is worth a Mass'?

 Culture & Belief — Under the new Pinyin language system for English speakers of Chinese, what is Peking known as?

 Stage & Screen — What future film director shot to fame as the dark-haired one in *Starsky and Hutch*?

 Written Word — Who did Sherlock Holmes rent his Baker Street rooms from?

 Music — Who had a hit in the US and Britain with *Achy Breaky Heart*?

 Famous People — Who was the last-surviving member of Hollywood's hard-living Rat Pack?

 Sport & Leisure — Which country first put up the yachting trophy, the America's Cup?

 Science & Tech — Where could you find The Microscope, The Clock and The Table?

 True or False? — A tympanum is a percussion instrument; true or false?

ANSWERS: PAGE 168

Food & Drink
Who said 'I do not like broccoli … I am president of the United States and I am not going to eat any more'?

 Natural World
In what modern-day country did the city of Troy lie?

 History
When, to the nearest 10 years, was the last time you could hire a climbing boy to clean your chimney?

 Culture & Belief
What is the world's most-spoken language?

 Stage & Screen
What film's publicity read 'Part man. Part machine. All cop'?

 Written Word
What book do Rat, Mole, Badger and Toad appear in?

 Music
What did William Blake want to build in England's green and pleasant land?

 Famous People
What king was called Old Rowley, after a famous stud stallion?

 Sport & Leisure
When was the first one-day international cricket match contested?

 Science & Tech
What would you expect to find in a body cavity?

 True or False?
Sculptures of Christ's crucifixion are known as calvaries; true or false?

ANSWERS: PAGE 168

What do the German Purity Laws of Reinheitsgebot regulate?

 How many millions of years have humans been on the Earth, to the nearest million?

 Who in 1966 were declared to be more popular than Jesus Christ?

 Calculate: the Plagues of Egypt plus Horsemen of the Apocalypse minus Tribes of Israel; how many are left?

 What actor played *The Wild One*?

 Who fell asleep in the Catskill Mountains for 20 years?

 What is the highest-pitched woodwind instrument?

 What traditionally male occupation did Grace O'Malley, Mary Read and Ann Bonny excel at?

 What are the colours of the five rings on the Olympic symbol?

 What is light amplification by stimulated emission of radiation better known as?

 The Hebrew alphabet has 44 letters; true or false?

ANSWERS: PAGE 169

Food & Drink
Where would you find a parson's nose?

 Natural World
In genetics, what do an x chromosome plus a y chromosome add up to?

 History
In what century did the potato arrive in Britain?

 Culture & Belief
What is the collective term for a group of judges?

 Stage & Screen
Three generations of the same family have all been Oscar winners; who are they?

 Written Word
Who said in his autobiography, *Goodbye To All That*?

 Music
Who wrote *Mad Dogs and Englishmen (Go Out In The Midday Sun)*?

 Famous People
How many Rolling Stones have there been?

 Sport & Leisure
What teams contested the first-recorded inter-county cricket match in 1709?

 Science & Tech
What is the name of the imaginary lines which encircle the Earth parallel to the Equator?

 True or False?
Appendicitis is very rare in Africa and Asia; true or false?

ANSWERS: PAGE 169

Food & Drink
What fruit is used to make calvados?

Natural World
What city was known as Edo before assuming its current name in 1868?

History
What was destroyed in Paris on 14th July 1789?

Culture & Belief
Who was Judas Iscariot's replacement?

Stage & Screen
What sit-com featured Frankie Howerd as a crafty Roman slave?

Written Word
In what Ian Fleming novel did James Bond make his first appearance?

Music
What rockabilly rebel recorded the album *Copperhead Road*?

Famous People
Mr Nelson and Ms Ciccone are rock stars better known by their first names; what are they?

Sport & Leisure
Which English football team has the largest pitch?

Science & Tech
Who was the first person to be killed by a train?

True or False?
Of the 626 people featured on the Bayeux Tapestry, none are women; true or false?

Food & Drink

What beer refreshed the parts other beers couldn't reach?

Natural World

What is the largest city in Europe?

History

Where was China's 1989 pro-democracy movement crushed by government troops?

Culture & Belief

What, according to Karl Marx, was the opium of the people?

Stage & Screen

What '80s TV character's catchphrase was 'Gissa job. I can do that'?

Written Word

Where could you hear the slogan 'All animals are equal but some animals are more equal than others'?

Music

In what operetta would you hear *He Is An Englishman*?

Famous People

What rock star's nickname is The Boss?

Sport & Leisure

What was unique about the White Heather Cricket Club founded at Nun Appleton in Yorkshire in 1887?

Science & Tech

What is the next number in the sequence: 2, 3, 5, 7, 11 … ?

True or False?

Barbers derive their name from the Berber peoples of North Africa; true or false?

ANSWERS: PAGE 170

Food & Drink What did Adolf Hitler ban on the day he proclaimed the Third Reich?

 Natural World What substance are lignite and anthracite forms of?

 History When, to the nearest 10 years, was the Louvre first opened to the public?

 Culture & Belief What is the most commonly used word in written English?

 Stage & Screen Who was the animator in *Monty Python's Flying Circus*?

 Written Word Who wrote *The Great Gatsby*?

 Music What song did Donny Osmond and Tab Hunter have in common?

 Famous People What famous child star later became US representative to the UN and ambassador to Ghana?

 Sport & Leisure Who scored England's goals in the 1966 World Cup Final?

 Science & Tech What was the first planet to be discovered by use of a telescope?

 True or False? A camel's hump is where it stores water; true or false?

ANSWERS: PAGE 171

Food & Drink

What is the traditional fare on Shrove Tuesday?

Natural World

What is the lowest area on the Earth's surface?

History

In what century were the first Olympic Games held in Greece?

Culture & Belief

What is the term for a painting done on a freshly plastered wall?

Stage & Screen

What does a best boy do on a film crew?

Written Word

Whose ghost haunted *Macbeth*?

Music

What US presidential candidate used Fleetwood Mac's *Don't Stop* as his campaign theme?

Famous People

By what title is the Earl of Inverness and Baron Killyleagh better known?

Sport & Leisure

What sport began in Holland, was later popularised in Scotland then dominated by Canada in modern times?

Science & Tech

What might you see if refraction occurred during precipitation?

True or False?

An 'oxbow' is the name of a type of knot; true or false?

ANSWERS: PAGE 171

Food & Drink — What raising agent is used in soda bread?

 Natural World — Meteorologically, what are the Doldrums?

 History — Which British monarch was crowned 11 years after he first became king?

 Culture & Belief — What is ironstone?

 Stage & Screen — What film was summarised by a critic as 'A building catches fire, some people die, some people don't'?

 Written Word — Who was King Arthur's wife?

 Music — What popular early-20th-century Irish–American singer was given a papal peerage?

 Famous People — What successful American portrait painter was also known for his dots and dashes?

 Sport & Leisure — Who was the first British footballer to be knighted?

 Science & Tech — In what century was the first city sewer built?

 True or False? — Piltdown Man was an archaeologically important pre-historic skull found in Sussex in 1912; true or false?

ANSWERS: PAGE 172

Food & Drink — What region of France does claret come from?

 Natural World — What is Europe's highest mountain?

 History — Why did American drinkers cry into their beer in January 1920?

 Culture & Belief — What would you be doing if you were performing an arabesque?

 Stage & Screen — What was the name of the bespectacled, intelligent, plain girl in *Scooby Doo*?

 Written Word — What was the first land Gulliver visited on his travels?

 Music — Who wrote *Mack The Knife*?

 Famous People — Who has been the only divorced president of the US?

 Sport & Leisure — When was the first Tour de France held?

 Science & Tech — How many spokes has a snowflake?

 True or False? — A panda is a member of the bear family; true or false?

ANSWERS: PAGE 172

Food & Drink
'Christmas is coming and ...' what are getting fat?

Natural World
What deadly disease was finally declared eradicated in 1980?

History
What other two countries joined the Common Market at the same time as the UK?

Culture & Belief
When do Spanish children receive their Christmas presents?

Stage & Screen
What Oscar-winning animator helped create Bugs Bunny, Daffy Duck and the Road Runner?

Written Word
What George Bernard Shaw play was the inspiration for the musical *My Fair Lady*?

Music
Who went to number 1 in the UK chart in 1972 with *Son Of My Father*?

Famous People
What nationality was T. S. Eliot?

Sport & Leisure
How many hoops are used in a game of croquet?

Science & Tech
What is the smallest constellation?

True or False?
If Force is measured in Newtons, the force of an apple dropping to the ground is roughly 1 Newton; true or false?

ANSWERS: PAGE 173

Food & Drink What puts the fizz in fizzy drinks?

 Natural World What trip did the book *The Worst Journey In The World* relate?

 History Why were London's journalists flushed with relief on 2nd February 1852?

 Culture & Belief What name are members of the Society of Jesus better known by?

 Stage & Screen What is the connection between Broccoli and James Bond?

 Written Word Who was Tom Sawyer's best friend?

 Music What military campaign did Tchaikovsky's *1812 Overture* celebrate?

 Famous People What colony, later to become a country, did Cecil Rhodes found?

 Sport & Leisure What was given to the British Open golf champion before the claret-jug trophy was introduced in 1872?

 Science & Tech In what decade was the first photograph taken?

 True or False? The word 'dunce' began as a term of abuse among followers of quarrelling medieval philosophers; true or false?

ANSWERS: PAGE 173

Food & Drink

What colour would you turn food if you added beta carotene to it?

Natural World

What is a death cap?

History

What faith was Henry VIII called the Defender of?

Culture & Belief

What peoples prefer to be known as Kooris?

Stage & Screen

What film KO'd the competition for Best Film Oscar in 1976?

Written Word

Who is the main character in the poem with the line 'Rats! They fought the dogs and killed the cats'?

Music

Who wrote and first performed the R & B classic *Johnny B. Goode*?

Famous People

Who said in 1982 'Mount Everest is now littered with junk from bottom to top'?

Sport & Leisure

What is the longest race in the world?

Science & Tech

How did the QWERTY keyboard get its name?

True or False?

Casanova was expelled from a seminary for alleged homosexuality; true or false?

ANSWERS: PAGE 174

Food & Drink
What beans are cooked to give baked beans?

Natural World
What animal was the first to be domesticated systematically?

History
What colour is the ribbon of the Victoria Cross?

Culture & Belief
What is the Pentateuch?

Stage & Screen
What de Gaulle lookalike was the star of *Jour de Fête* and *Monsieur Hulot's Holiday*?

Written Word
What king's three daughters were Goneril, Regan and Cordelia?

Music
What musical monarch was said to have penned the tune *Greensleeves*?

Famous People
Who is unique in modern Europe as the only man to have founded his own church and political party?

Sport & Leisure
The Grand National, the Laurels and the Scurry Gold Cup are all classic races for what animals?

Science & Tech
Where would you find the Sea of Tranquillity?

True or False?
Vladimir Heavy Draught is a Russian beer; true or false?

ANSWERS: PAGE 174

Food & Drink What is arrowroot most commonly used for?

 Natural World What is Britain's only poisonous snake?

 History What Conservative said 'We must build a kind of United States of Europe'?

 Culture & Belief Roman, Gothic, Ogee and Horseshoe are all types of what?

 Stage & Screen What was Frederico Fellini's 1959 vision of the sweet life in Rome?

 Written Word What book, written in the 1920s, was the subject of an obscenity trial when finally published in 1960?

 Music What rock legend was the subject of Don McLean's *American Pie*?

 Famous People Who once ferried people across Niagara Falls on a high-wire wheelbarrow?

 Sport & Leisure What does 'karate' mean?

 Science & Tech What planet's orbit takes it nearest to Earth?

 True or False? Spiders do not belong to the insect world; true or false?

ANSWERS: PAGE 175

Food & Drink
What is sucrose more commonly known as?

 Natural World
What species outnumber all others on Earth put together?

 History
Who described life in the Royal Navy as 'rum, sodomy and the lash'?

 Culture & Belief
What was unusual about the Gorgons' hairstyles?

 Stage & Screen
What Japanese film classic was *The Magnificent Seven* based on?

 Written Word
Who wrote *The Ballad Of The Sad Café*?

 Music
What fairy tale did the original Engelbert Humperdinck set to music?

 Famous People
What poet and diabolist claimed to be the Beast from the Book of Revelation?

 Sport & Leisure
In what four disciplines do women gymnasts compete in competition?

 Science & Tech
What is toxicology the study of?

 True or False?
The flags of Poland and Indonesia are identical; true or false?

ANSWERS: PAGE 175

Food & Drink — What additive is thought to cause Chinese Restaurant Syndrome?

Natural World — What century did the common dodo become extinct in?

History — Who was killed on the Ides of March?

Culture & Belief — What 1955 design in glass by Raymond Loewy is now a classic?

Stage & Screen — What Ingmar Bergman film sees a knight playing chess with Death to prolong his own life?

Written Word — What novel won the Booker Prize for Salman Rushdie?

Music — Who scored a two-time hit with his *Shotgun Wedding*?

Famous People — Whose nickname was The Welsh Wizard?

Sport & Leisure — Which country is the home of hurling?

Science & Tech — Which has the shorter wavelength – light waves or radio waves?

True or False? — No mammal can fly (except in an aeroplane); true or false?

ANSWERS: PAGE 176

Food & Drink Why is royal jelly so called?

 Natural World How much blood is in the average human adult body?

 History What US president was said not to be able to fart and chew gum at the same time?

 Culture & Belief What is the highest rank in the Royal Navy?

 Stage & Screen Who did Robert de Niro portray in his Oscar-winning performance in *Raging Bull*?

 Written Word What poet drowned in the Mediterranean near Viareggio in August 1822?

 Music Who did Cab Calloway call 'a low-down hoochie-coocher'?

 Famous People What was Greek artist Domenikos Theotokopoulos better known as?

 Sport & Leisure India and Pakistan between them won the gold medal in what sport at every Olympics from 1928 to 1968?

 Science & Tech What was the Earth's first artificial satellite?

 True or False? Guests at the world's only underwater hotel in Florida have to scuba-dive to their rooms; true or false?

ANSWERS: PAGE 176

Food & Drink What drink is made from molasses?

 Natural World Where is the Great Barrier Reef?

 History What was the official title of the Poll Tax?

 Culture & Belief What design style did the 1925 Exposition des Arts Décoratifs in Paris give rise to?

 Stage & Screen Who promised 'I'll be back'?

 Written Word Who was the deformed sexton in Victor Hugo's *Notre Dame De Paris*?

 Music Who wrote *The Mighty Quinn*?

 Famous People Who was the last Hanoverian monarch of Britain?

 Sport & Leisure Greco–Roman and Freestyle are the two main types of which sport?

 Science & Tech What is a CAT scanner generally used to find?

 True or False? Buffalo Bill once kicked off a football match at Glasgow's Hampden Park; true or false?

ANSWERS: PAGE 177

Food & Drink What are prunes before they are dried?

 Natural World What makes a humming bird hum?

 History How many Cinque Ports were there?

 Culture & Belief What 1931 design by Henry C. Beck unravelled a maze for Londoners?

 Stage & Screen What words appear on the scroll beneath the MGM lion?

 Written Word What newspaper did Clark Kent write for?

 Music What famous song is set to the music of Elgar's *Pomp and Circumstance March No. 1*?

 Famous People Who did Mark Antony appoint king of the Jews?

 Sport & Leisure The Edmonton Oilers, the Chicago Black Hawks and the Toronto Maple Leafs compete in what sport?

 Science & Tech What satellite passed Jupiter in 1979, Saturn in 1981, Uranus in 1986 and Neptune in 1989?

True or False? Over 350 separate languages have been officially recorded in the tiny kingdom of Tonga; true or false?

ANSWERS: PAGE 177

Food & Drink
What pudding was named after an Australian opera singer?

 Natural World
What islands did Darwin visit to get evidence in support of his theories of natural selection?

 History
Who did Margaret Thatcher feel she could do business with in 1984?

 Culture & Belief
What country used *The Internationale* as its national anthem until 1944?

 Stage & Screen
Who played The Artful Dodger in the 1968 film musical *Oliver!*?

 Written Word
What writer of the macabre penned *The Fall Of The House Of Usher* and *The Masque Of The Red Death*?

 Music
What campaigning singer–songwriter wrote and performed *Cats In The Cradle*?

 Famous People
What famous jazz singer was known as 'Lady Day'?

 Sport & Leisure
Which was the first European team to win football's World Cup?

 Science & Tech
What is measured by an anemometer?

 True or False?
Guy Fawkes was trying to blow up the House of Commons; true or false?

ANSWERS: PAGE 178

Food & Drink — What did Jesus do at the Cana wedding feast?

 Natural World — How many chromosomes are in a normal human body cell?

 History — What Prime Minister gave Britain the three-day week?

 Culture & Belief — What do American babies wear on their bottoms?

 Stage & Screen — Name two of the three films which have won Oscars for animator Nick Parks.

 Written Word — What was the name of Bertie Wooster's club?

 Music — Who, according to Robert Burns' song, did the deil, or devil, dance away with?

 Famous People — What small item is Alec Issigonis famous for designing?

 Sport & Leisure — How many players does a Gaelic Football team have?

 Science & Tech — What recurrent stellar visitor to Earth was featured on the Bayeux Tapestry?

True or False? — The Morris Mini was the first British car to sell one million; true or false?

ANSWERS: PAGE 178

Food & Drink — What red meat has the lowest fat content?

 Natural World — What animal's name means 'river horse'?

 History — What was the relationship between Indian prime ministers Jawaharlal Nehru and Indira Gandhi?

 Culture & Belief — Where can the Wallace Monument be found?

 Stage & Screen — Who played Dr Kildare in the long-running '60s TV series?

 Written Word — What million-selling book caused Alexander Solzhenitsyn's deportation from the USSR in 1973?

 Music — What Viennese father and son were renowned masters of the waltz?

 Famous People — What did the 'F' in JFK stand for?

 Sport & Leisure — What is the highest possible judo grade?

 Science & Tech — What man-made vehicle holds the all-time speed record?

 True or False? — Nitrogen is the second-biggest component of the air we breathe; true or false?

ANSWERS: PAGE 179

Food & Drink
How many people did Jesus feed with five loaves and two fish?

 Natural World
How long, to the nearest metre, is the adult human small intestine?

 History
What president called his country 'a rainbow nation at peace with itself and the world'?

 Culture & Belief
What notorious Mormon church leader was a polygamist with reputedly over 50 wives?

 Stage & Screen
What musical featured the songs *Surrey With The Fringe On Top* and *Oh What A Beautiful Morning*?

 Written Word
Who wrote *Brighton Rock*?

 Music
What musician and producer did Cait O'Riordan leave the Pogues to marry?

 Famous People
What two famous Irishmen were involved in the biggest sex scandals of the Victorian era in Britain?

 Sport & Leisure
In what sport would you find a foil and an épée?

 Science & Tech
What is the common name of iron pyrites?

 True or False?
A constellation called Norma can be seen from the Southern Hemisphere; true or false?

Food & Drink What cake is traditionally eaten on Easter Sunday?

 Natural World What unit of measurement was King Henry I's arm used to define?

 History Which university is older – Oxford or Cambridge?

 Culture & Belief How many pints of beer would you expect from a flagon?

 Stage & Screen What political group featured in Leni Riefenstahl's film *Triumph Of The Will*?

 Written Word What was William Wordsworth describing when he wrote 'Earth hath not anything to show more fair'?

 Music What big-band leader popularised 'swing' in 1935?

 Famous People Whose nickname was The Desert Fox?

 Sport & Leisure What is the racquet used in lacrosse called?

 Science & Tech If a submarine submerged to 10 fathoms, how far below the surface would it be?

True or False? Croissants were first made by French bakers to celebrate a victory in battle over the Turks; true or false?

ANSWERS: PAGE 180

Food & Drink
What are Java, Columbian and Kenyan?

Natural World
If diamond is the hardest mineral, what is the softest?

History
Who offered a New Deal to the American nation during the Depression?

Culture & Belief
Which part of a ship is the Union Jack flown from – front or back?

Stage & Screen
What cult American TV show was always introduced by its creator, Rod Serling?

Written Word
Name the Three Musketeers.

Music
What, according to Brendan Behan, 'went jingle-jangle all along the banks of the Royal Canal'?

Famous People
Who announced his retirement by saying that he wanted to get out with his greatness intact?

Sport & Leisure
What newspaper originally sponsored the Tour of Britain Milk Race for cyclists?

Science & Tech
What substance causes plants to be green?

True or False?
A booklouse is someone who reads books excessively; true or false?

ANSWERS: PAGE 180

Food & Drink
Which contains more caffeine – coffee beans or tea leaves?

Natural World
What period of Earth's history came first – Jurassic or Carboniferous?

History
What are the Tower of London's Yeomen of the Guard better known as?

Culture & Belief
What was St Paul's trade?

Stage & Screen
What *Dallas* regular first made his name playing opposite a genie in *I Dream of Jeannie*?

Written Word
How did James Joyce immortalise 16th June 1904, the day he first 'walked out' with his future wife, Nora?

Music
What song, originally by Lord Rockingham's XI, was used in a wine-gums commercial in the mid 1990s?

Famous People
Who is fourth in line to the British throne?

Sport & Leisure
Who is the most-capped Scottish footballer?

Science & Tech
What Apollo space mission put the first men on the Moon?

True or False?
Sir Walter Raleigh invented an early form of the bicycle; true or false?

ANSWERS: PAGE 181

Food & Drink
What would you be eating if you had a toad in the hole?

 Natural World
At what angle does the Earth tilt towards the Sun?

 History
What did Melbourne, Derby and Aberdeen have in common?

 Culture & Belief
What is the oldest cathedral in Britain?

 Stage & Screen
What was the name of the Ewings' ranch in *Dallas*?

 Written Word
What was the name of Bill Sikes' dog in *Oliver Twist*?

 Music
What American DJ first coined the term 'rock-and-roll music'?

 Famous People
What princess won a gold disc for a duet with Bing Crosby?

 Sport & Leisure
Besides lawn tennis, what sport has its English headquarters at Wimbledon?

 Science & Tech
What is trinitrotoluene better known as?

 True or False?
Margaret Thatcher's tenure of office was the longest of any woman prime minister; true or false?

ANSWERS: PAGE 181

Food & Drink
What fruit was traditionally eaten on Mothering Sunday and Palm Sunday?

 Natural World
What is the speed of sound at ground level?

 History
What king was encouraged by a spider's perseverance to try and try again?

 Culture & Belief
Who was the American continent named after?

 Stage & Screen
What island was the home of detective Jim Bergerac?

 Written Word
What two travellers went *Around The World In Eighty Days*?

 Music
According to the carol, of all the trees that are in the wood, which one bears the crown?

 Famous People
What was the connection between Chang and Eng?

 Sport & Leisure
How many players are there in a water polo team?

 Science & Tech
What is the process used to split atomic particles and create massive energy release?

 True or False?
Rock Around The Clock was the first single to sell more than one million copies; true or false?

ANSWERS: PAGE 182

Food & Drink
What make up the three layers in Millionaire's Shortcake?

Natural World
What part of Oliver Cromwell's body was found at his post-mortem to be almost twice the normal size?

History
What did Hannibal cross the Alps for?

Culture & Belief
Which country has more schools than any other?

Stage & Screen
Who was *To The Manor Born*?

Written Word
What bear of very little brain lived in the Hundred Acre Wood?

Music
What Barry McGuire tune topped the chart for the protest movement in 1965?

Famous People
What teen idol shot to fame in 1970 with the Partridge Family?

Sport & Leisure
What game was originally known as 'kitten ball'?

Science & Tech
Copper, zinc and what other metal make up German silver?

True or False?
Tony Blackburn presented the first edition of *Top Of The Pops*; true or false?

ANSWERS: PAGE 182

Food & Drink
What are hash browns?

 Natural World
Who swore before the Inquisition that the Earth revolved around the Sun?

 History
What renowned sailor and explorer lies in a watery grave off Panama?

 Culture & Belief
If a Welshman added pump and pum cant together, what would be the total?

 Stage & Screen
What holiday camp catchphrase was the title of an '80s sitcom?

 Written Word
According to Oscar Wilde, what type of man knows the price of everything and the value of nothing?

 Music
Whose persona was Ziggy Stardust?

 Famous People
Who led the Prague Spring in 1968?

 Sport & Leisure
Which three sports feature in the triathlon?

 Science & Tech
What was it that drove hatters mad?

 True or False?
The soft drink Kia-Ora takes its name from the Maori word for 'good health'; true or false?

ANSWERS: PAGE 183

Food & Drink
How much is in a punnet?

Natural World
What makes the Bolivian city of La Paz virtually fireproof?

History
What aquatic event took place off Griffin's Wharf in Boston Harbour, 1773?

Culture & Belief
What city is called after the Greek goddess Athene?

Stage & Screen
Who played the voice of the baby in *Look Who's Talking*?

Written Word
Who was *Lady Chatterley's Lover*?

Music
Who declared *Je Ne Regrette Rien*?

Famous People
What was Second World War radio announcer William Joyce better known as?

Sport & Leisure
What was the first north European team to win football's European Cup?

Science & Tech
What is an imaginary number?

True or False?
The bowie knife was invented by the famous American frontiersman Jim Bowie; true or false?

ANSWERS: PAGE 183

Food & Drink
What fruit is used to flavour Aurum liqueur?

Natural World
What does a hippophile have a particular interest in?

History
What year did the *Mayflower* arrive in America?

Culture & Belief
What is the English translation of the French word 'cocorico'?

Stage & Screen
Who took the title role in *I, Claudius*?

Written Word
What grew in the garden of *Mary, Mary, Quite Contrary*?

Music
What group's name was inspired by Keith Moon's verdict that they would go down like a lead balloon?

Famous People
Who was the last viceroy of India?

Sport & Leisure
Where is elephant soccer played?

Science & Tech
What name is given to a person whose body lacks melanin?

True or False?
The Isle of Man was the first place to give women the vote; true or false?

ANSWERS: PAGE 184

Food & Drink
What is frangipane?

 Natural World
What nature-loving saint is the patron of ecologists?

 History
Who led the Free French government in exile during the Second World War?

 Culture & Belief
How many letters are used in the world's shortest alphabet, on the Solomon Islands?

 Stage & Screen
What soap is set around events on Ramsay Street?

 Written Word
Who was the bemused, planet-hopping hero of *The Hitch-Hiker's Guide To The Galaxy*?

 Music
Who was called the Queen of Soul?

 Famous People
By what name is the 15th-century Balkan leader Vlad the Impaler immortalised in literature?

 Sport & Leisure
Where is the World Professional Snooker Championship played?

 Science & Tech
What did alchemists strive to do?

 True or False?
John F. Kennedy was the youngest-ever US president; true or false?

ANSWERS: PAGE 184

Food & Drink

Where did chocolate originate?

Natural World

What mythical undersea land was known as the lost continent?

History

What prime minister did Winston Churchill describe as 'a modest man with much to be modest about'?

Culture & Belief

Who did J. B. S. Haldane call 'the greatest Jew since Jesus'?

Stage & Screen

What do *The Young Ones*, *The Thin Blue Line* and *Blackadder* all have in common?

Written Word

What medieval Italian civil servant made his own name a by-word for cynicism with his book, *The Prince*?

Music

What group of supposed brothers was at the forefront of punk with *Sheena Is A Punk Rocker*?

Famous People

1978 was the year of the Three Popes – who were they?

Sport & Leisure

Which English Premiership team began life as Dial Square FC?

Science & Tech

Along with protons and electrons, what other particle goes to make up atoms?

True or False?

Blood group O negative is the commonest blood type in the UK; true or false?

ANSWERS: PAGE 185

Food & Drink
Which are generally hotter – green or red chillis?

 Natural World
What function does the human appendix perform?

 History
What political party introduced the old-age pension?

 Culture & Belief
Who dreamt of a ladder, changed his name and fathered 12 children to lead Israel's 12 tribes?

 Stage & Screen
What '70s US drama featured a family living through the Depression in Virginia's Blue Ridge Mountains?

 Written Word
What did the famous Sun headline 'Gotcha' refer to?

 Music
According to the song, what did I spy on the streets of Laredo?

 Famous People
What politician's criticisms were likened to being savaged by a dead sheep?

 Sport & Leisure
In what sport is the Camanachd Cup the premier competition?

 Science & Tech
If oxygen is O^2, what is O^3?

 True or False?
Queen Victoria was the first European monarch to use a telephone; true or false?

ANSWERS: PAGE 185

Food & Drink
What is haslet?

Natural World
Name two of the four creatures that the Bible says were sent to plague the Egyptians.

History
Why did the prime minister and cabinet end up under the table in 10 Downing Street on 7th February 1991?

Culture & Belief
What do bungalows, pundits and verandahs all have in common?

Stage & Screen
What famous film director makes a cameo appearance at the end of *The Blues Brothers*?

Written Word
What famous children's tale features a Canadian orphan called Anne Shirley?

Music
At what event were all the ants fancy-dancing with the fleas?

Famous People
Who said 'A man in the house is worth two in the street'?

Sport & Leisure
How many countries did the 1996 Tour de France pass through?

Science & Tech
How many bytes are there in a kilobyte of computer memory?

True or False?
William Caxton invented the printing press; true or false?

ANSWERS: PAGE 186

Food & Drink
What did the Aztecs cut off what they called the testicle tree?

 Natural World
What did Peter hear after he had disowned Jesus three times?

 History
When, to within five years, were driving tests introduced in Britain?

 Culture & Belief
What would an Irishman do with a boreen?

 Stage & Screen
What is a clapper board used for?

 Written Word
What document was described as 'the longest suicide note in history'?

 Music
What rock-and-roll quartet was the first white act to play Harlem's Apollo Theatre?

 Famous People
What Nazi war criminal sentenced at Nuremberg served the longest sentence?

 Sport & Leisure
What was the UEFA Cup originally known as?

 Science & Tech
What common ailment can be cured by acetylsalicylic acid?

 True or False?
The first vacuum cleaner was so large that it was horse-drawn and could not get inside houses; true or false?

ANSWERS: PAGE 186

Food & Drink
What did Oliver Twist ask for more of?

Natural World
What is the southernmost point in the British Isles?

History
How did John Hinckley try to impress Jodie Foster in 1981?

Culture & Belief
If livestock is a farmer's animals, what is dead stock?

Stage & Screen
What is the name of Postman Pat's black-and-white cat?

Written Word
What poet was described as 'Mad, bad, and dangerous to know'?

Music
Who is the more famous brother of Mike McGear of The Scaffold?

Famous People
Irishman Arthur Wellesley gave his name to what type of footwear?

Sport & Leisure
What colour is Mayfair on a Monopoly board?

Science & Tech
What organ in the body produces insulin?

True or False?
Chinese typewriter keyboards have around 1500 characters; true or false?

ANSWERS: PAGE 187

Food & Drink

What spirit is made from potatoes?

Natural World

What is the biggest lake in Britain?

History

Who were Churchill's Few?

Culture & Belief

What Chinese philosopher was so revered he was worshipped as a god?

Stage & Screen

Which famous '60s pop star provided the TV voice of *Thomas the Tank Engine*?

Written Word

Who wrote *The First Blast Of The Trumpet Against The Monstrous Regiment Of Women*?

Music

Where was the Tamla Motown record company first established?

Famous People

Why did Rolls-Royce change their car's badge colour from red to black?

Sport & Leisure

What tournament was thought up in 1955 by Gabriel Hanot, soccer editor of French newspaper *L'Equipe*?

Science & Tech

What road-safety device was invented by Percy Shaw in 1934?

True or False?

The Caesarean section operation was named after Julius Caesar who was thought to have been born that way; true or false?

ANSWERS: PAGE 187

Food & Drink What vegetable are G.I.s credited with introducing to Britain?

 Natural World What is normally the longest-lived animal?

 History In what year did the Bank of England replace pound notes with coins?

 Culture & Belief What is the British name of the organisation known as Little Bees in Switzerland and Ladybirds in Italy

 Stage & Screen Who was the proprietor of *Fawlty Towers*?

 Written Word Who wrote *One Hundred Years Of Solitude*?

 Music What is the name Motown short for?

 Famous People Who was the first music star to be screamed at by young fans?

 Sport & Leisure What are the colours of the three jerseys awarded during the Tour de France?

 Science & Tech Cheriton in Britain and Sargette in France have a common link – what is it?

 True or False? As well as cuckoo birds, cuckoo bees also exist; true or false?

ANSWERS: PAGE 188

Food & Drink
What vegetable did Mark Twain describe as 'Cabbage with a college education'?

 Natural World
What mammal has webbed feet, a duck-like bill and lays eggs?

 History
Who said, 'A week is a long time in politics'?

 Culture & Belief
What island was King Arthur taken to after being wounded in his final battle?

 Stage & Screen
Who was the guiding hand behind Kermit the Frog and Miss Piggy?

 Written Word
Who was *Down And Out In Paris And London*?

 Music
Who composed the music for such blockbusters as *Star Wars*, *Superman* and *Raiders Of The Lost Ark*?

 Famous People
What famous singer starred in the world's first talkie?

 Sport & Leisure
What do cyclists feel when they hit the 'bonk'?

 Science & Tech
What freezes to form 'dry ice'?

 True or False?
The socialist republicans were the rebels in the Spanish Civil War; true or false?

ANSWERS: PAGE 188

Food & Drink — What are Ben and Jerry known for?

 Natural World — What birds eat, sleep and breed on the wing?

 History — What event does the children's rhyme *Ring-A-Ring O' Roses* commemorate?

 Culture & Belief — Who was the Apostle of the Gentiles?

 Stage & Screen — What cult US TV show launched the careers of Steve Martin, Bill Murray, John Belushi and Dan Aykroyd?

 Written Word — Who did Sherlock Holmes describe as 'The Napoleon of Crime'?

 Music — What instrument did Glenn Miller play?

 Famous People — Whose nickname was 'The Little Tramp'?

 Sport & Leisure — What are the discs used in tiddlywinks called?

 Science & Tech — What is a computer's footprint?

 True or False? — Stonefish is the name of a type of coral; true or false?

ANSWERS: PAGE 189

Food & Drink — What is glorious about August 12th?

 Natural World — How many capitals does South Africa have?

 History — In what country did the sauna originate?

 Culture & Belief — What three saints' crosses are represented on the Union Flag?

 Stage & Screen — What were the names of the Flowerpot Men?

 Written Word — Where did Professor Moriarty meet his death at the hands of Sherlock Holmes?

 Music — What member of *Monty Python's Flying Circus* provided the theme song for *One Foot In The Grave*?

 Famous People — Who led the famous Dambusters raid during the Second World War?

 Sport & Leisure — What Scottish pastime did Hugh Munro give his name to?

 Science & Tech — Where would you find a lancet, a galilee and a finial?

 True or False? — The tibia bone's connected to the radius bone; true or false?

ANSWERS: PAGE 189

What Italian pudding's name translates as 'Pick-me-up'?

 In what modern-day country is the ancient city of Petra?

 What did Vincent van Gogh do after quarrelling with Paul Gauguin?

 What do Hindus and Buddhists call the state of oneness with god?

 What real-life brothers played the Kray Twins on film?

 Who ended his nightly diary entries with the words, 'And so to bed'?

 Who was George Michael's partner in Wham!?

 Who was lead singer of the group Nirvana?

 Who was the first BBC Sports Personality Of The Year?

 What are Doric, Ionic and Corinthian all types of?

 Kellogg first developed breakfast cereals in 1906 as a health food for psychiatric patients; true or false?

ANSWERS: PAGE 190

Food & Drink — To what profession of Frenchman would you give a *pourboire* (literally meaning 'for drinking')?

Natural World — Which Scottish county's main town lies in another country?

History — Which country was Montezuma ruler of?

Culture & Belief — What is Montezuma's Revenge?

Stage & Screen — Who played *The Blues Brothers*?

Written Word — Whose political views were set out in the book entitled *My Struggle*?

Music — Who was *Kissing With Confidence* in 1983?

Famous People — What famous model of the '60s was known as The Shrimp?

Sport & Leisure — Who missed the penalty that put England out of the 1996 European Championships?

Science & Tech — How many ounces to the pound are there in the troy system?

True or False? — A carillon is the specific name given to a chorister in Canterbury Cathedral; true or false?

ANSWERS: PAGE 190

SECTION TWO

THE QUIZ BOOK ANSWERS

SETS 1 – 120

SET 1

Food & Drink	A poisoned apple
Natural World	Mad Cow Disease
History	Two
Culture & Belief	Eros
Stage & Screen	Four

Written Word	Melchester
Music	The road to Mandalay
Famous People	Arthur Miller and Marilyn Monroe
Sport & Leisure	For winning the US Masters and leading the Tour de France
Science & Tech	Stephen Hawking
True or False?	True

SET 2

Food & Drink	Manna
Natural World	Four inches
History	Caligula
Culture & Belief	Christian Dior
Stage & Screen	Z Cars

Written Word	The Canterbury Tales
Music	Beethoven
Famous People	Allan Pinkerton
Sport & Leisure	Kirkcaldy
Science & Tech	Karl Benz
True or False?	True

SET 3

Food & Drink
Juniper

Natural World
Chicago

History
To sound less German in WWI (it was a name-change)

Culture & Belief
Ecuador (they were shipped from Panama)

Stage & Screen
North By Northwest

Written Word
John Osborne

Music
Noel Gallagher

Famous People
Charles Darwin

Sport & Leisure
Pot Black

Science & Tech
On the side of a ship

True or False?
True

SET 4

Food & Drink
Fat

Natural World
The Negev

History
Almost 29 years (1961–89)

Culture & Belief
Quakers

Stage & Screen
Snow White And The Seven Dwarfs

Written Word
The four archangels

Music
Leon Trotsky

Famous People
Paul Keating

Sport & Leisure
New Zealand

Science & Tech
Albert Einstein

True or False?
False (it did in 1877)

SET 5

		Written Word	Erskine Childers
Food & Drink	A cheese	Music	*Reasons To Be Cheerful, Part 3*
Natural World	The Northern Lights	Famous People	Aviation
History	None	Sport & Leisure	The Jules Rimet Trophy
Culture & Belief	The Ten Commandments	Science & Tech	The de Haviland Comet
Stage & Screen	Charlton Heston	True or False?	True (in 1892)

SET 6

		Written Word	Silas Marner
Food & Drink	Smash Instant Mashed Potato	Music	A miner 49-er
Natural World	Aurora australis	Famous People	Work
History	26	Sport & Leisure	1972
Culture & Belief	Drink from it	Science & Tech	Dynamite
Stage & Screen	The nickname of India's film industry	True or False?	False (the Queen has no passport)

SET 7

Written Word		Ophelia	

| Food & Drink | Turmeric | Music | Richie Valens and The Big Bopper |

| Natural World | The River Nile | Famous People | Wallis Simpson |

| History | Julius Caesar | Sport & Leisure | 100 m, 200 m, 4 x 100 m relay, Long Jump |

| Culture & Belief | 15th March | Science & Tech | Jacques Cousteau |

| Stage & Screen | Jacques Cousteau's | True or False? | False (the casualty tally was reversed) |

SET 8

| Written Word | | Ebenezer Scrooge |

| Food & Drink | Herring | Music | Pete Best |

| Natural World | Pennsylvania | Famous People | Walt Disney |

| History | Sarajevo | Sport & Leisure | Thomas Lord (its developer) |

| Culture & Belief | Capricorn | Science & Tech | All known chemical elements |

| Stage & Screen | Pinky And Perky | True or False? | True |

SET 9

Food & Drink	Bitter
Natural World	The intestines of sheep
History	Abraham Lincoln
Culture & Belief	Demons and goblins
Stage & Screen	Scott, Virgil, Alan, Gordon, John

Written Word	Mycroft
Music	*Flowers In The Rain* (by The Move)
Famous People	All were assassinated
Sport & Leisure	India
Science & Tech	The Morris Mini
True or False?	False (all are types of knot)

SET 10

Food & Drink	Haggis
Natural World	A reindeer
History	1863
Culture & Belief	The pope
Stage & Screen	Fred Astaire and Ginger Rogers

Written Word	Salome
Music	Tennessee
Famous People	All were left handed
Sport & Leisure	35–1
Science & Tech	Uranus
True or False?	False (there are 9)

SET 11

Food & Drink	Ham and cheese
Natural World	A meteor
History	The Library of Alexandria
Culture & Belief	£50
Stage & Screen	Toto

Written Word	Manchester
Music	Louis Armstrong
Famous People	Satchel-mouth
Sport & Leisure	Kenneth Wolstenholme (at the World Cup Final)
Science & Tech	By being the first woman in space
True or False?	True

SET 12

Food & Drink	Beans Means Heinz
Natural World	The River Nile
History	Countess Constance Markievicz (in 1918)
Culture & Belief	St Valentine
Stage & Screen	George C. Scott and Marlon Brando

Written Word	Billy Bunter
Music	T'Pau
Famous People	Louis XIV (by 8 years)
Sport & Leisure	Dennis Taylor
Science & Tech	The Humber Bridge
True or False?	True

SET 13

Written Word		Harry Lime	
Food & Drink	Honey	Music	*Rockin' All Over The World* (by Status Quo)
Natural World	K2	Famous People	Orson Welles'
History	The First World War ended	Sport & Leisure	Uruguay (in 1930)
Culture & Belief	Ten	Science & Tech	John Glenn
Stage & Screen	Fred Astaire	True or False?	True

SET 14

Written Word		Matt Groening	
Food & Drink	Jerusalem artichokes	Music	The Chieftains
Natural World	Shipping areas	Famous People	Canterbury Cathedral
History	James VI of Scotland and I of England	Sport & Leisure	Scrabble
Culture & Belief	So be it	Science & Tech	Just over 8 minutes
Stage & Screen	Celia Johnson and Trevor Howard	True or False?	True

SET 15

Food & Drink	In a hot dog roll
Natural World	Texas
History	Lady Jane Grey (queen for 10 days)
Culture & Belief	The Koran
Stage & Screen	The 4th of July

Written Word	Superman (by 11 months)
Music	The Jordanaires
Famous People	US President Theodore Roosevelt
Sport & Leisure	A pack of cards
Science & Tech	Your knee-cap
True or False?	False

SET 16

Food & Drink	Coca-Cola
Natural World	Canberra
History	The Confederacy
Culture & Belief	Hope
Stage & Screen	St Elmo's Fire

Written Word	Smallville
Music	Wagner
Famous People	Andrew Carnegie
Sport & Leisure	Weightlifting
Science & Tech	DNA
True or False?	False

SET 17

Food & Drink — A lemon

Natural World — Greenland

History — Seven

Culture & Belief — 25th March, year 0

Stage & Screen — *The White Horses*

Written Word — George Orwell

Music — Both had hits with *Amazing Grace*

Famous People — Václav Havel

Sport & Leisure — Scotland and England

Science & Tech — The structure of DNA

True or False? — True

SET 18

Food & Drink — Marie Antoinette

Natural World — Vatican City

History — Hyde Park

Culture & Belief — Taoism

Stage & Screen — Mr Benn

Written Word — Lewis Carroll

Music — New York

Famous People — Andy Warhol

Sport & Leisure — Tourist Trophy

Science & Tech — Pasteurisation

True or False? — False

SET 19

 Written Word — George Bernard Shaw

 Food & Drink — Whisky (meaning 'water of life')

 Music — Harry Lauder

 Natural World — Poland

 Famous People — Buzz Aldrin

 History — The Great Exhibition of 1851

 Sport & Leisure — Trevor Francis

 Culture & Belief — The Mormon Church

 Science & Tech — Each was named after its inventor

 Stage & Screen — Weatherfield

 True or False? — True

SET 20

 Written Word — *How To Win Friends & Influence People*

 Food & Drink — In meat pies (his neighbour was a baker)

 Music — Sarah Brightman

 Natural World — None (they are two names for the same animal)

 Famous People — Florence Nightingale

History — Franklin D. Roosevelt

 Sport & Leisure — 47 minutes

 Culture & Belief — Haile Selassie

 Science & Tech — 1001

Stage & Screen — The Archers

 True or False? — False

SET 21

Food & Drink	Aubergine
Natural World	The fast speed of its beating wings
History	Richard Cromwell
Culture & Belief	Hinduism
Stage & Screen	The Archers
Written Word	Ronald Reagan
Music	Simon Rattle
Famous People	Charles Stewart Parnell
Sport & Leisure	1984 (Los Angeles)
Science & Tech	Rust
True or False?	False (it is Mandarin)

SET 22

Food & Drink	Sherry
Natural World	20,000
History	The crown jewels
Culture & Belief	The pyramids of Egypt
Stage & Screen	*Catweazle*
Written Word	Bash Street
Music	*Galway Bay*
Famous People	Roald Amundsen
Sport & Leisure	Joe Di Maggio
Science & Tech	90 degrees
True or False?	False

SET 23

Food & Drink
A folded-over pizza

Natural World
Cape Town

History
His arm

Culture & Belief
Chinese culture

Stage & Screen
Eldorado

Written Word
The Barretts

Music
A septet

Famous People
Uri Geller

Sport & Leisure
Boris Becker

Science & Tech
1919

True or False?
True

SET 24

Food & Drink
Robert Louis Stevenson

Natural World
Feign death to fool your opponent

History
George VI

Culture & Belief
In the centre (it is where the congregation sits)

Stage & Screen
Camberwick Green

Written Word
C. S. Lewis

Music
The Overlanders

Famous People
Paul Revere

Sport & Leisure
Samuel Beckett

Science & Tech
Helium

True or False?
True

SET 25

Food & Drink	Potatoes
Natural World	A blue whale calf
History	4 July 1976
Culture & Belief	Abel
Stage & Screen	Eugene O'Neill
Written Word	Wilfred Owen
Music	Billy Ocean
Famous People	Madonna
Sport & Leisure	Jamaica
Science & Tech	The compact disc
True or False?	False (it blooms every 10–30 years)

SET 26

Food & Drink	Prawns
Natural World	Istanbul
History	US troops in Britain in WWII
Culture & Belief	David
Stage & Screen	Flipper and Skippy
Written Word	Gnasher
Music	Andy Stewart
Famous People	Oscar Wilde
Sport & Leisure	Athens (in 1896)
Science & Tech	Viruses
True or False?	True

SET 27

Food & Drink — The Greek gods

Natural World — Nepal

History — Culloden

Culture & Belief — Coca-Cola's

Stage & Screen — Tennessee Williams

Written Word — *A La Recherche Du Temps Perdu* (by Marcel Proust)

Music — Blur

Famous People — Billy Graham

Sport & Leisure — 22

Science & Tech — 32

True or False? — False (it was curry)

SET 28

Food & Drink — A marinated herring

Natural World — The Great Wall of China

History — The IRA (after the Brighton bombing)

Culture & Belief — King Arthur

Stage & Screen — The Capulets

Written Word — King Arthur

Music — Eric Clapton

Famous People — Little

Sport & Leisure — The British Empire Games

Science & Tech — The gluteus maximus

True or False? — True

SET 29

Food & Drink	Lemon
Natural World	The USSR
History	The Order of the Garter
Culture & Belief	Buddha
Stage & Screen	*Breakfast At Tiffany's*
Written Word	Big Ears
Music	Eight maids a-milking
Famous People	Jean Harlow
Sport & Leisure	1968
Science & Tech	None (it is a bell)
True or False?	True

SET 30

Food & Drink	They are all champagne-bottle sizes
Natural World	Brambles
History	1968
Culture & Belief	Teacher
Stage & Screen	Cap. Jean-Luc Picard (in *Star Trek: The Next Generation*)
Written Word	12
Music	Luciano Pavarotti, José Carreras and Placido Domingo
Famous People	Marilyn Monroe
Sport & Leisure	Princess Anne
Science & Tech	Albert Einstein
True or False?	True

SET 31

Food & Drink	Garibaldi	**Written Word**	Walter Scott
Natural World	Everything	**Music**	*The Gambler*
History	Alaska	**Famous People**	Fidel Castro
Culture & Belief	One (French)	**Sport & Leisure**	Bjorn Borg
Stage & Screen	*Father Ted*	**Science & Tech**	$^{22}/_{7}$
		True or False?	False (it was a chair-back cover)

SET 32

Food & Drink	Picnic baskets	**Written Word**	Flo
Natural World	A depression or low	**Music**	Daniel Barenboim
History	One	**Famous People**	Mother Theresa of Calcutta
Culture & Belief	A US dollar bill	**Sport & Leisure**	The High Jump
Stage & Screen	He is an android	**Science & Tech**	Robert Oppenheimer
		True or False?	True

SET 33

		Written Word	Yukio Mishima
Food & Drink	Beer	Music	Pluck
Natural World	Cirrus	Famous People	July
History	Suffragettes	Sport & Leisure	The Harlem Globetrotters
Culture & Belief	Esso's	Science & Tech	The elbow
Stage & Screen	*Cabaret*	True or False?	True

SET 34

		Written Word	*The Addams Family*
Food & Drink	Anna Pavlova	Music	Finger its holes to play notes
Natural World	Approx. 3960 miles (6385 km)	Famous People	Bonnie Prince Charlie
History	The prime minister	Sport & Leisure	The Triathlon
Culture & Belief	Woodstock	Science & Tech	Surgery
Stage & Screen	Mulder and Scully	True or False?	False (it was 1914)

SET 35

Food & Drink	Locusts and wild honey
Natural World	Fingerprints
History	Six
Culture & Belief	St Augustine
Stage & Screen	Victor Meldrew
Written Word	Ursula Le Guin
Music	Babylon Zoo
Famous People	William Randolph Hearst
Sport & Leisure	Yachting
Science & Tech	212 degrees
True or False?	True

SET 36

Food & Drink	Almond
Natural World	Lava is magma which comes onto the Earth's surface
History	The Battle of Waterloo
Culture & Belief	Christopher Wren
Stage & Screen	*Northern Exposure*
Written Word	The Falklands War
Music	John Brown's
Famous People	Ike Turner (she is Tina)
Sport & Leisure	Geoff Hurst
Science & Tech	Four
True or False?	False (he only worked in South Africa)

SET 37

Food & Drink	Haggis
Natural World	Four
History	Black and blue
Culture & Belief	The Weathermen
Stage & Screen	Emergency Room

Written Word	Lord Of The Flies
Music	The Kinks
Famous People	Che Guevara
Sport & Leisure	In the USA
Science & Tech	Too low
True or False?	False (it is a region in Argentina)

SET 38

Food & Drink	Three years
Natural World	Lakes
History	William the Conqueror
Culture & Belief	To show membership of a club
Stage & Screen	Hopkirk was a ghost

Written Word	In Xanadu
Music	Giacomo Puccini
Famous People	Boadicea
Sport & Leisure	2000 Guineas, Derby, St Leger
Science & Tech	The liver
True or False?	True

SET 39

Food & Drink	Gelatine
Natural World	15 degrees
History	Albania
Culture & Belief	Scientology
Stage & Screen	*Cheers*
Written Word	Paris and London
Music	Garth Brooks
Famous People	Edward VII
Sport & Leisure	Featherweight
Science & Tech	Yeast
True or False?	True

SET 40

Food & Drink	Roast lamb
Natural World	ante meridiem and post meridiem
History	Damascus
Culture & Belief	Riverdance
Stage & Screen	*Friends*
Written Word	Oscar Wilde
Music	ABC
Famous People	Billy the Kid
Sport & Leisure	Bobby Jones
Science & Tech	Red
True or False?	False

SET 41

Food & Drink	Currency
Natural World	Australia and New Zealand
History	1984
Culture & Belief	The pope
Stage & Screen	Brideshead
Written Word	*The Hitch-Hiker's Guide To The Galaxy*
Music	Phil Lynott
Famous People	Pat Garrett
Sport & Leisure	All have hosted the Commonwealth Games
Science & Tech	Mercury
True or False?	False (the only one who did was Nixon)

SET 42

Food & Drink	Bread
Natural World	Aluminium
History	The *Titanic*
Culture & Belief	Martin Luther King
Stage & Screen	*True Grit*
Written Word	His pipe, bowl and fiddlers three
Music	Johnny Cash
Famous People	Andrew Carnegie
Sport & Leisure	London and Glasgow
Science & Tech	Two
True or False?	False

SET 43

Food & Drink	Months without an 'r' in them
Natural World	Chalk
History	1920s
Culture & Belief	240
Stage & Screen	*Dad's Army*
Written Word	He died
Music	*My Generation*
Famous People	David Lloyd George
Sport & Leisure	Basketball
Science & Tech	Atmosphere
True or False?	False

SET 44

Food & Drink	It is unleavened
Natural World	Winds
History	His right
Culture & Belief	Stephen
Stage & Screen	It was the first colour TV series
Written Word	A secret never to be told
Music	Culture Club
Famous People	F. W. Woolworth
Sport & Leisure	The F. A. Cup
Science & Tech	Twice the speed of sound
True or False?	False

SET 45

Food & Drink	Jonah
Natural World	Alaska
History	John F. Kennedy
Culture & Belief	Saatchi & Saatchi
Stage & Screen	Fay Wray
Written Word	It's the temperature books combust at
Music	Erasure
Famous People	Gerald Ford
Sport & Leisure	Pelota
Science & Tech	273.15
True or False?	True

SET 46

Food & Drink	It's raw
Natural World	The International Date Line
History	Tax evasion
Culture & Belief	Fair Isle knitwear
Stage & Screen	*Star Trek*
Written Word	Haggis
Music	Richie Valens, Los Lobos
Famous People	The Red Baron
Sport & Leisure	72
Science & Tech	Tin
True or False?	True

SET 47

Food & Drink	Pea soup
Natural World	Fog
History	Sitting Bull
Culture & Belief	Quangos
Stage & Screen	Silver

Written Word	Three
Music	A cappella
Famous People	Sleep (he suffered from insomnia)
Sport & Leisure	Polo
Science & Tech	An imperial ton
True or False?	True

SET 48

Food & Drink	Seaweed
Natural World	2062
History	Britain (in the Boer War)
Culture & Belief	In the Old Testament
Stage & Screen	*Steamboat Willie*

Written Word	Arthur Miller
Music	Elvis Presley (with 8 in 1957)
Famous People	George III
Sport & Leisure	Saïd Aouita
Science & Tech	An earthquake
True or False?	True

SET 49

Food & Drink	Texas
Natural World	The Navaho
History	A UFO
Culture & Belief	Baked earth
Stage & Screen	Corleone
Written Word	J. M. Synge
Music	*We Shall Overcome*
Famous People	Rasputin
Sport & Leisure	Lacrosse
Science & Tech	Upper arm bone and buttock muscle
True or False?	True

SET 50

Food & Drink	Oats
Natural World	The Angel Falls in Venezuela
History	Robert Peel
Culture & Belief	Paper money (it is a wallet)
Stage & Screen	They are uncle and nephew
Written Word	Mario Puzo
Music	*The Bells Of Hell*
Famous People	Lawrence of Arabia
Sport & Leisure	26 miles 385 yd
Science & Tech	60 degrees
True or False?	True

SET 51

		Written Word	Brendan Behan
Food & Drink	Cow pie	**Music**	A solo performance
Natural World	The African elephant	**Famous People**	Vivienne Westwood
History	Government Issue	**Sport & Leisure**	A bamboo sword
Culture & Belief	St Swithin	**Science & Tech**	To prevent them freezing (it is anti-freeze)
Stage & Screen	*In Which We Serve*	**True or False?**	False (Scotch comes only from Scotland)

SET 52

		Written Word	Robert Burns
Food & Drink	Sugar and spice and all things nice	**Music**	*Carmen*
Natural World	Thailand	**Famous People**	Henry Ford
History	China	**Sport & Leisure**	Ice
Culture & Belief	A girl's coming of age	**Science & Tech**	A nautical mile
Stage & Screen	*Dr Zhivago*	**True or False?**	False (it is a 12-sided regular polygon)

SET 53

Food & Drink	1930s	Written Word	The Simpsons
Natural World	The Moon's gravitational pull	Music	The Sex Pistols
History	Shergar	Famous People	William Wallace and Robert Burns
Culture & Belief	Matthew	Sport & Leisure	30
Stage & Screen	*Breakfast At Tiffany's*	Science & Tech	35
		True or False?	True

SET 54

Food & Drink	A Bath Oliver	Written Word	Homer
Natural World	20 square feet	Music	*Cats*
History	1801	Famous People	Jeremy Bentham
Culture & Belief	The Salvation Army	Sport & Leisure	Boston
Stage & Screen	The Simon Park Orchestra	Science & Tech	Four
		True or False?	True

SET 55

Food & Drink	William Pitt the Younger
Natural World	Two (Scotland and England)
History	The *Queen Mary* and *QEII*
Culture & Belief	The mini-skirt
Stage & Screen	Commander, Royal Navy

Written Word	James Joyce
Music	Abba's
Famous People	Matt Busby
Sport & Leisure	St Leger
Science & Tech	Strengthens it
True or False?	False (it was Chicago)

SET 56

Food & Drink	Tea
Natural World	Seven
History	Maundy Money
Culture & Belief	And the rest
Stage & Screen	Huey Lewis

Written Word	Percy Bysshe Shelley
Music	Scott Joplin
Famous People	Michael Flatley
Sport & Leisure	Baseball
Science & Tech	The elevator
True or False?	True

SET 57

Written Word	Artistotle
Food & Drink	A tandoor (or clay oven)
Music	*Miss Saigon*
Natural World	Scafell Pike
Famous People	Timothy Leary
History	The privatisation of public assets
Sport & Leisure	Epsom
Culture & Belief	In the trunk
Science & Tech	Vitamin C
Stage & Screen	John Wayne
True or False?	True

SET 58

Written Word	Winston Churchill
Food & Drink	Fish and chips (they are salt and vinegar)
Music	D'Oyly Carte
Natural World	Connacht, Ulster, Munster, Leinster
Famous People	Margaret Thatcher
History	Texan Governor John Connolly
Sport & Leisure	Baltimore
Culture & Belief	The Book of Revelation
Science & Tech	Oranges
Stage & Screen	*Some Like It Hot*
True or False?	True

SET 59

Food & Drink	None (it's a fish)
Natural World	Belfast
History	The American railroad
Culture & Belief	Franz Hals
Stage & Screen	*Murder By Decree*
Written Word	*The Taming Of The Shrew*
Music	*Super Trooper*
Famous People	Mama Cass Elliot
Sport & Leisure	Augusta National Couse, Georgia
Science & Tech	A rainbow
True or False?	False (it was William Olds)

SET 60

Food & Drink	In a distillery
Natural World	J. J. Audubon
History	The Crimean War
Culture & Belief	Your grace
Stage & Screen	Both were played by David Prowse
Written Word	Flashman
Music	Between two operatic scenes or acts
Famous People	John Lennon
Sport & Leisure	Cross-country skiing and rifle shooting
Science & Tech	Red and blue
True or False?	False

SET 61

Written Word			Sancho Panza
Food & Drink	Curry-flavoured soup	**Music**	*My Favourite Things*
Natural World	Newly qualified doctors	**Famous People**	Heather Locklear
History	Pudding Lane	**Sport & Leisure**	Three
Culture & Belief	25th March	**Science & Tech**	Hardness
Stage & Screen	*Ben Hur*	**True or False?**	True

SET 62

Written Word			Domesday Book
Food & Drink	The USA	**Music**	Amen Corner
Natural World	Oxygen and nitrogen	**Famous People**	Ray Harryhausen
History	The League of Nations	**Sport & Leisure**	Bowling
Culture & Belief	The Royal Navy	**Science & Tech**	Syphilis
Stage & Screen	Marlon Brando and Robert De Niro	**True or False?**	True

SET 63

Food & Drink	Bovril
Natural World	The South Pole
History	Richard Nixon
Culture & Belief	Henry VIII
Stage & Screen	John Ford

Written Word	Dante Alighierii
Music	A fever
Famous People	Richard Lester
Sport & Leisure	Oxford
Science & Tech	An apple falling on his head
True or False?	False

SET 64

Food & Drink	Cocoa beans
Natural World	Penicillin
History	Eamon de Valera
Culture & Belief	True love
Stage & Screen	A Clockwork Orange

Written Word	Anthony Burgess
Music	Very loud
Famous People	Emma Thompson
Sport & Leisure	Joe Frasier and George Foreman
Science & Tech	'What You See Is What You Get'
True or False?	True

SET 65

Food & Drink	An egg

Natural World	Greenfly

History	Chaim Herzog

Culture & Belief	12

Stage & Screen	Oscar Hammerstein

Written Word	The Restaurant At The End Of The Universe

Music	The Eagle

Famous People	Clark Gable

Sport & Leisure	24 hours

Science & Tech	88

True or False?	False

SET 66

Food & Drink	Bows

Natural World	Donegal

History	Napoleon

Culture & Belief	The *Argo*

Stage & Screen	A Matter Of Life And Death

Written Word	Robert Burns'

Music	*My Old Man*

Famous People	Tommy Cooper's

Sport & Leisure	64

Science & Tech	In the ear (it is 1 mm long)

True or False?	True

SET 67

Food & Drink	It does not signify anything	**Written Word**	Delilah
Natural World	Ayers Rock	**Music**	When it is sung all the way through
History	Dan Quayle	**Famous People**	John F. Kennedy's
Culture & Belief	Faith, hope, charity, prudence, fortitude, justice, temperance	**Sport & Leisure**	Skiing
Stage & Screen	Sergio Leone	**Science & Tech**	Veteran
		True or False?	False (it is a shrewdness)

SET 68

Food & Drink	Thanksgiving	**Written Word**	He was staked through the heart and beheaded
Natural World	Nectar and pollen	**Music**	Country & Western
History	116 years (1337–1453)	**Famous People**	Sid Vicious
Culture & Belief	Pride, gluttony, lust, anger, sloth, envy, covetousness	**Sport & Leisure**	England and Australia
Stage & Screen	*High Noon*	**Science & Tech**	Another diamond
		True or False?	False (Britain has no written constitution)

SET 69

Food & Drink	Tonic water
Natural World	The albatross (4 m)
History	H. H. Kitchener
Culture & Belief	8 days
Stage & Screen	*Escape To Victory*
Written Word	*Whisky Galore*
Music	Vince Hill
Famous People	Fatty Arbuckle
Sport & Leisure	Jimmy White
Science & Tech	Lies
True or False?	False

SET 70

Food & Drink	The first is Scotch; the other isn't
Natural World	The peregrine (112 mph)
History	The Napoleonic Wars
Culture & Belief	Pentecost
Stage & Screen	*The Quiet Man*
Written Word	*Kidnapped* and *Catriona*
Music	Keep the red flag flying here
Famous People	Phil Spector
Sport & Leisure	Gary Sobers
Science & Tech	24
True or False?	False (it was Mr Goodyear)

SET 71

Food & Drink	432
Natural World	Bread
History	King Edward I
Culture & Belief	1,788
Stage & Screen	Wimbledon Common
Written Word	The Arabian Nights Entertainment
Music	The book of the performance
Famous People	Elvis Costello
Sport & Leisure	Korea
Science & Tech	30 stone
True or False?	True

SET 72

Food & Drink	William Kellogg
Natural World	Burma
History	Four
Culture & Belief	Vietnam
Stage & Screen	The Poseidon Adventure
Written Word	The Dead Sea Scrolls
Music	Julio Iglesias
Famous People	33
Sport & Leisure	Kayak and Canadian
Science & Tech	Away from it
True or False?	False (fire needs air to burn)

SET 73

Food & Drink
The Earl of Sandwich

Natural World
The North Sea and the Baltic

History
It was stolen from Westminster Abbey

Culture & Belief
Red

Stage & Screen
Rear Window

Written Word
Knitting

Music
Dolly Parton and Whitney Houston

Famous People
Adolf Hitler

Sport & Leisure
French & Australian championships, US Open, Wimbledon

Science & Tech
In the air

True or False?
True

SET 74

Food & Drink
A herring

Natural World
It has no tail

History
Israel beat Egypt, Jordan and Syria

Culture & Belief
Mancunium

Stage & Screen
It's A Wonderful Life

Written Word
Mrs Rochester

Music
Line dancing

Famous People
Anna Pavlova

Sport & Leisure
Russia

Science & Tech
Adrenalin

True or False?
True

SET 75

Food & Drink	Caviare
Natural World	Beijing
History	Henri IV
Culture & Belief	Beijing
Stage & Screen	Paul Michael Glaser
Written Word	Mrs Hudson
Music	Billy Ray Cyrus
Famous People	Frank Sinatra
Sport & Leisure	England
Science & Tech	In the sky (they are constellations)
True or False?	False (it is an architectural feature)

SET 76

Food & Drink	George Bush
Natural World	Turkey
History	1840
Culture & Belief	Mandarin
Stage & Screen	*Robocop*
Written Word	*Wind In The Willows*
Music	Jerusalem
Famous People	Charles II
Sport & Leisure	1971
Science & Tech	The body's vital organs
True or False?	True

SET 77

Food & Drink	German beer
Natural World	Four
History	The Beatles
Culture & Belief	2 (10 + 4 − 12)
Stage & Screen	Marlon Brando
Written Word	Rip Van Winkle
Music	The piccolo
Famous People	Piracy
Sport & Leisure	Yellow. red, black, blue, green
Science & Tech	Laser
True or False?	False (it has 22)

SET 78

Food & Drink	On a chicken
Natural World	A boy
History	The 16th century
Culture & Belief	A bench
Stage & Screen	Walter, John and Angelica Huston
Written Word	Robert Graves
Music	Noël Coward
Famous People	7
Sport & Leisure	Kent and Surrey
Science & Tech	Lines of latitude
True or False?	True

SET 79

Written Word	*Casino Royale*
Food & Drink	Apples
Music	Steve Earle
Natural World	Tokyo
Famous People	Prince and Madonna
History	The Bastille prison
Sport & Leisure	Manchester City
Culture & Belief	Matthias
Science & Tech	William Huskisson MP, Trade Secretary
Stage & Screen	*Up Pompeii*
True or False?	False (3 are)

SET 80

Written Word	*Animal Farm*
Food & Drink	Heineken
Music	*HMS Pinafore*
Natural World	Moscow
Famous People	Bruce Springsteen
History	Tiananmen Square
Sport & Leisure	It was the first women's cricket club
Culture & Belief	Religion
Science & Tech	13 (they are prime numbers)
Stage & Screen	Yosser Hughes (in *Boys From The Blackstuff*)
True or False?	False

SET 81

Food & Drink	Kosher food
Natural World	Coal
History	1793
Culture & Belief	The
Stage & Screen	Terry Gilliam

Written Word	F. Scott Fitzgerald
Music	*Young Love*
Famous People	Shirley Temple
Sport & Leisure	Martin Peters and Geoff Hurst (3)
Science & Tech	Uranus
True or False?	False

SET 82

Food & Drink	Pancakes
Natural World	The Mariana Trench
History	The eighth century
Culture & Belief	A fresco
Stage & Screen	He is assistant to the senior electrician

Written Word	Banquo's
Music	Bill Clinton
Famous People	The Duke of York
Sport & Leisure	Curling
Science & Tech	A rainbow
True or False?	False (it is a type of lake)

SET 83

Food & Drink	Bicarbonate of soda
Natural World	Light Equatorial winds
History	Charles II
Culture & Belief	A type of pottery
Stage & Screen	*The Towering Inferno*

Written Word	Guinevere
Music	John McCormack
Famous People	Samuel Morse
Sport & Leisure	Stanley Matthews
Science & Tech	6th century BC (in Rome)
True or False?	False (it was a fake)

SET 84

Food & Drink	Bordeaux
Natural World	Elbrus
History	Prohibition on alcohol sales began
Culture & Belief	Ballet dancing
Stage & Screen	Velma

Written Word	Lilliput
Music	Kurt Weill and Bertolt Brecht
Famous People	Ronald Reagan
Sport & Leisure	1903
Science & Tech	Six
True or False?	False (it is closely related to raccoons)

SET 85

Food & Drink	The geese
Natural World	Smallpox
History	Ireland and Denmark
Culture & Belief	6th January (Feast of the Three Kings)
Stage & Screen	Chuck Jones
Written Word	Pygmalion
Music	Chicory Tip
Famous People	American
Sport & Leisure	6
Science & Tech	The Southern Cross
True or False?	True

SET 86

Food & Drink	Carbon dioxide
Natural World	Captain Scott's South Pole voyage
History	Britain's first flushing public toilets opened on Fleet St
Culture & Belief	Jesuits
Stage & Screen	'Cubby' Broccoli produced the Bond movies
Written Word	Huckleberry Finn
Music	Napoleon's retreat from Moscow
Famous People	Rhodesia (now Zimbabwe)
Sport & Leisure	A championship belt
Science & Tech	1820s
True or False?	True

SET 87

Food & Drink	Orange
Natural World	A deadly toadstool
History	Catholicism
Culture & Belief	Australian Aborigines
Stage & Screen	*Rocky*

Written Word	*The Pied Piper of Hamelin*
Music	Chuck Berry
Famous People	Edmund Hillary
Sport & Leisure	The Whitbread Round-The World Yacht Race
Science & Tech	From its first six letter keys
True or False?	True

SET 88

Food & Drink	Haricot beans
Natural World	The dog
History	Maroon
Culture & Belief	The first five books of the Bible
Stage & Screen	Jacques Tati

Written Word	King Lear
Music	Henry VIII
Famous People	Ian Paisley
Sport & Leisure	Greyhounds
Science & Tech	On the Moon
True or False?	False (it is a Russian horse)

SET 89

Food & Drink	A thickener
Natural World	The adder
History	Winston Churchill
Culture & Belief	Arches
Stage & Screen	*La Dolce Vita*
Written Word	*Lady Chatterley's Lover*
Music	Buddy Holly
Famous People	Charles Blondin
Sport & Leisure	'Empty hand'
Science & Tech	Venus'
True or False?	True

SET 90

Food & Drink	Sugar
Natural World	Insects
History	Winston Churchill
Culture & Belief	They had live snakes for hair
Stage & Screen	*The Seven Samurai*
Written Word	Carson McCullers
Music	*Hansel And Gretel*
Famous People	Aleister Crowley
Sport & Leisure	Asymmetrical bars, beam, horse-vault, floor exercises
Science & Tech	Poisons
True or False?	False (they have the same colours, but reversed)

SET 91

Food & Drink — Monosodium glutamate

Natural World — The 17th century

History — Julius Caesar

Culture & Belief — The Coca-Cola bottle

Stage & Screen — *The Seventh Seal*

Written Word — *Midnight's Children*

Music — Roy 'C'

Famous People — Lloyd George

Sport & Leisure — Ireland

Science & Tech — Light waves

True or False? — False (bats can fly)

SET 92

Food & Drink — It is fed by workers to queen bees

Natural World — 5 litres (8 pints)

History — Gerald Ford

Culture & Belief — Admiral of the Fleet

Stage & Screen — Jake La Motta

Written Word — Percy Bysshe Shelley

Music — *Minnie The Moocher*

Famous People — El Greco

Sport & Leisure — Hockey

Science & Tech — Sputnik 1

True or False? — True

SET 93

Food & Drink	Rum
Natural World	Off Australia's north-east coast
History	The Community Charge
Culture & Belief	Art Deco
Stage & Screen	*The Terminator*
Written Word	Quasimodo
Music	Bob Dylan
Famous People	Victoria
Sport & Leisure	Wrestling
Science & Tech	Cancers in the human body
True or False?	True

SET 94

Food & Drink	Plums
Natural World	The speed of its wings beating
History	Seven
Culture & Belief	The London Underground map
Stage & Screen	Ars Gratia Artis
Written Word	*The Daily Planet*
Music	*Land Of Hope And Glory*
Famous People	Herod the Great
Sport & Leisure	Ice Hockey
Science & Tech	Voyager 2
True or False?	False

SET 95

Food & Drink
Peach Melba (after Nellie Melba)

Natural World
The Galapagos Islands

History
Mikhail Gorbachev

Culture & Belief
The USSR

Stage & Screen
Jack Wild

Written Word
Edgar Allan Poe

Music
Harry Chapin

Famous People
Billie Holiday

Sport & Leisure
Italy

Science & Tech
Wind speed

True or False?
False (it was the House of Lords)

SET 96

Food & Drink
Changed water into wine

Natural World
46

History
Edward Heath

Culture & Belief
Diapers

Stage & Screen
Creature Comforts, A Close Shave, The Wrong Trousers

Written Word
The Drones

Music
The exciseman

Famous People
The Morris Mini

Sport & Leisure
15

Science & Tech
Halley's Comet

True or False?
False (it was the Morris Minor)

SET 97

Food & Drink	Veal	**Written Word**	*The Gulag Archipelago*
Natural World	Hippopotamus	**Music**	Johann Strauss I and II
History	They were father and daughter	**Famous People**	Fitzgerald
Culture & Belief	Stirling	**Sport & Leisure**	12th dan
Stage & Screen	Richard Chamberlain	**Science & Tech**	Apollo 10 (at 39,897 kph)
		True or False?	False (it is the biggest)

SET 98

Food & Drink	5000	**Written Word**	Graham Greene
Natural World	Six metres	**Music**	Elvis Costello
History	Nelson Mandela	**Famous People**	Oscar Wilde and Charles Stewart Parnell
Culture & Belief	Brigham Young	**Sport & Leisure**	Fencing
Stage & Screen	*Oklahoma!*	**Science & Tech**	Fool's gold
		True or False?	True

SET 99

Food & Drink	Simnel cake
Natural World	A yard
History	Oxford
Culture & Belief	Two
Stage & Screen	The Nazi party
Written Word	London
Music	Benny Goodman
Famous People	Erwin Rommel
Sport & Leisure	A crosse
Science & Tech	60 ft
True or False?	True

SET 100

Food & Drink	Types of coffee
Natural World	Talc
History	President Franklin D. Roosevelt
Culture & Belief	The front (or bow)
Stage & Screen	*The Twilight Zone*
Written Word	Athos, Porthos and Aramis
Music	*The Old Triangle*
Famous People	Muhammad Ali
Sport & Leisure	*The Daily Express*
Science & Tech	Chlorophyll
True or False?	False (it is an insect which eats book bindings))

SET 101

Food & Drink
Tea leaves

Natural World
Carboniferous

History
Beefeaters

Culture & Belief
A tent-maker

Stage & Screen
Larry Hagman

Written Word
By setting all the action in *Ulysses* on that day

Music
Hoots Mon

Famous People
The Duke of York

Sport & Leisure
Kenny Dalglish

Science & Tech
Apollo 11

True or False?
False

SET 102

Food & Drink
Sausages baked in batter

Natural World
$23\frac{1}{2}$ degrees

History
All were British prime ministers

Culture & Belief
Canterbury

Stage & Screen
Southfork

Written Word
Bull's-Eye

Music
Alan Freed

Famous People
Princess Grace (Grace Kelly)

Sport & Leisure
Croquet

Science & Tech
TNT

True or False?
False (Indira Gandhi held office longer over two terms)

SET 103

Food & Drink — Figs

Natural World — 760 mph (1200 kph)

History — Robert the Bruce

Culture & Belief — Amerigo Vespucci

Stage & Screen — Jersey

Written Word — Phileas Fogg and Passepartout

Music — The holly

Famous People — They were the original Siamese twins

Sport & Leisure — 7

Science & Tech — Nuclear fission

True or False? — True

SET 104

Food & Drink — Shortbread, caramel and chocolate

Natural World — His brain

History — To defeat the Romans in battle

Culture & Belief — China

Stage & Screen — Penelope Keith

Written Word — Winnie-the-Pooh

Music — *Eve Of Destruction*

Famous People — David Cassidy

Sport & Leisure — Softball

Science & Tech — Nickel

True or False? — False (it was Jimmy Saville)

SET 105

Food & Drink	Fried onion and potato cakes

Natural World	Galileo

History	Sir Francis Drake

Culture & Belief	505 (5 + 500)

Stage & Screen	*Hi-De-Hi*

Written Word	A cynic

Music	David Bowie's

Famous People	Alexander Dubcek

Sport & Leisure	Long-distance cycling, swimming and running

Science & Tech	The mercury used in hat manufacture

True or False?	True

SET 106

Food & Drink	There is no legal definition

Natural World	Its 3630 m altitude lacks the oxygen to sustain a large fire

History	The Boston Tea Party

Culture & Belief	Athens

Stage & Screen	Bruce Willis

Written Word	Mellors (the game-keeper)

Music	Edith Piaf

Famous People	Lord Haw-Haw

Sport & Leisure	Celtic

Science & Tech	The square root of a negative number

True or False?	False (it was his brother, Rezin; Jim only popularised it)

SET 107

Food & Drink	Orange
Natural World	Horses
History	1620
Culture & Belief	Cock-a-doodle-doo
Stage & Screen	Derek Jacobi
Written Word	Silver bells, cockle shells and pretty maids all in a row
Music	Led Zeppelin
Famous People	Lord Louis Mountbatten
Sport & Leisure	Thailand
Science & Tech	An albino
True or False?	True (in 1880)

SET 108

Food & Drink	Almond-flavoured paste (for cakes)
Natural World	Francis of Assisi
History	Charles de Gaulle
Culture & Belief	11
Stage & Screen	*Neighbours*
Written Word	Arthur Dent
Music	Aretha Franklin
Famous People	Count Dracula
Sport & Leisure	The Crucible Theatre, Sheffield
Science & Tech	Turn base metals into gold
True or False?	False (At 43, Teddy Roosevelt was a year younger)

SET 109

Food & Drink	Mexico
Natural World	Atlantis
History	Clement Attlee
Culture & Belief	Albert Einstein
Stage & Screen	All were written by Ben Elton

Written Word	Niccolò Machiavelli
Music	The Ramones
Famous People	Paul VI, John Paul I and John Paul II
Sport & Leisure	Arsenal
Science & Tech	Neutrons
True or False?	False (it is O positive)

SET 110

Food & Drink	Green
Natural World	It performs no function
History	The Liberals
Culture & Belief	Jacob
Stage & Screen	*The Waltons*

Written Word	The sinking of the Argentinian battleship *Belgrano*
Music	A young cowboy all wrapped in white linen
Famous People	Geoffrey Howe
Sport & Leisure	Shinty
Science & Tech	Ozone
True or False?	True (on 14th January 1878)

SET 111

Food & Drink — Pig-offal loaf

Natural World — Frogs, gnats, flies, locusts

History — The IRA launched a mortar attack on the building

Culture & Belief — All are originally Indian words

Stage & Screen — Steven Spielberg

Written Word — Anne Of Green Gables

Music — The Ugly Bugs' Ball

Famous People — Mae West

Sport & Leisure — 5 (France, Holland, Belgium, Italy, Spain)

Science & Tech — 1024

True or False? — False (it was Johannes Gutenberg)

SET 112

Food & Drink — Avocadoes

Natural World — A cock crowing

History — 1934

Culture & Belief — Walk along it

Stage & Screen — To synchronise sound and action in a scene

Written Word — The 1983 Labour Party election manifesto

Music — Buddy Holly and The Crickets

Famous People — Rudolf Hess

Sport & Leisure — The Fairs Cup

Science & Tech — A headache (it is aspirin)

True or False? — True

SET 113

Food & Drink	Gruel
Natural World	Lizard Point, Cornwall
History	He shot President Reagan
Culture & Belief	Farm equipment
Stage & Screen	Jess
Written Word	Lord Byron
Music	Paul McCartney
Famous People	The Wellington (he was the duke)
Sport & Leisure	Dark blue
Science & Tech	The pancreas
True or False?	True

SET 114

Food & Drink	Vodka
Natural World	Loch Lomond
History	The pilots who fought the Battle of Britain
Culture & Belief	Confucius
Stage & Screen	Ringo Starr
Written Word	John Knox
Music	Detroit, Michigan
Famous People	To mark the death of Henry Royce
Sport & Leisure	The European Champion Clubs' Cup
Science & Tech	Cats' eyes
True or False?	True

SET 115

			Written Word	Gabriel Garcia Marquez

Food & Drink	Sweetcorn		Music	Motor Town (Detroit is a major car-production centre)
Natural World	The tortoise (at 80+ years)		Famous People	Frank Sinatra
History	1988		Sport & Leisure	Green, yellow and white with red polka dots
Culture & Belief	The Guides		Science & Tech	The Channel Tunnel
Stage & Screen	Basil Fawlty		True or False?	True

SET 116

			Written Word	George Orwell

Food & Drink	Cauliflower		Music	John Williams
Natural World	The duck-billed platypus		Famous People	Al Jolson
History	Harold Wilson		Sport & Leisure	Extreme fatigue (it's the cyclists' 'pain barrier')
Culture & Belief	Avalon		Science & Tech	Carbon Dioxide
Stage & Screen	Jim Henson		True or False?	False (they were the government)

SET 117

Written Word	Moriarty

Food & Drink	Ice-cream
Music	Trombone

Natural World	Swifts
Famous People	Charlie Chaplin's

History	The Great Plague
Sport & Leisure	Winks

Culture & Belief	Paul
Science & Tech	The amount of space it occupies on a surface

Stage & Screen	*Saturday Night Live*
True or False?	False (it is a fish)

SET 118

Written Word	The Reichenbach Falls

Food & Drink	It is the start of the grouse-shooting season
Music	Eric Idle

Natural World	3 for different functions (Bloemfontein, Cape Town, Pretoria)
Famous People	Guy Gibson

History	Finland
Sport & Leisure	Munro-bagging (climbing mountains over 3000 ft)

Culture & Belief	St George, St Andrew, St Patrick
Science & Tech	On a church (they are parts of the building)

Stage & Screen	Bill and Ben
True or False?	False

SET 119

Food & Drink	Tiramisù
Natural World	Jordan
History	Cut off part of his ear
Culture & Belief	Nirvana
Stage & Screen	Martin and Gary Kemp
Written Word	Samuel Pepys
Music	Andrew Ridgeley
Famous People	Kurt Cobain
Sport & Leisure	Christopher Chataway
Science & Tech	Architectural columns
True or False?	True

SET 120

Food & Drink	A waiter (it is a tip)
Natural World	Berwickshire (Berwick is in England)
History	Mexico
Culture & Belief	The infectious diarrhoea suffered by tourists in Mexico
Stage & Screen	John Belushi and Dan Aykroyd
Written Word	Adolf Hitler
Music	Will Powers
Famous People	Jean Shrimpton
Sport & Leisure	Gareth Southgate
Science & Tech	20
True or False?	False; it is a set of bells hung in a tower